TAPESTRY OF A WALDORF CURRICULUM

A TEACHER'S GUIDE TO THE WALDORF SCHOOL

Grades 1–12

Tobias Richter
Editor

Tapestry of a Waldorf Curriculum
A Teacher's Guide to the Waldorf School
Grades 1–12

Edited by Tobias Richter

4th edition, enlarged and revised, 2016

Tobias Richter, born in 1948, attended the Waldorf School in his German hometown of Ulm before going on to study education in Reutlingen and Freiburg. After completing his Waldorf teacher training in Stuttgart, he taught both elementary and high school grades at the Rudolf Steiner School in Mauer, a suburb of Vienna, from 1972 to 1991. Since 1980 he has been active in Waldorf teacher education in Austria, Germany, and Croatia.

Published under the joint auspices of the Pädagogische Forschungsstelle beim Bund der Freien Waldorfschulen and the International Forum for Steiner/Waldorf Education (Hague Circle)

First issued in 1995 as a draft manuscript by the Pädagogische Forschungsstelle beim Bund der Freien Waldorfschulen. All texts by Rudolf Steiner are copyright by the Rudolf Steiner-Nachlassverwaltung, Dornach/Switzerland and published here with permission.

Translated by Norman Skillen

Waldorf Publications
ISBN 978-1-943582-38-9

All rights reserved. Printed in the United States of America. No part of this research may be used or reproduced in any manner without written permission except in the case of brief quotations in critical articles and reviews or in the case of schools recognized by the Association of Waldorf Schools of North America (AWSNA).

Copyright © 2020 by Waldorf Publications
at the Research Institute for Waldorf Education (RIWE)
351 Fairview Avenue, Unit 625
Hudson, NY 12534
www.waldorfresearchinstitute.org

For purchase at www.WaldorfPublications.org

Waldorf PUBLICATIONS

TABLE OF CONTENTS

Preface to the English Edition v
Foreword 1
On the Publication of this Guide 5

Part I
Tasks and Objectives of Waldorf Education 9

   1   The First Waldorf School 11
   2   The Curriculum in its Anthroposophical Context 13
   3   Administration through Community Participation 21
   4   Teaching and Learning Processes 27
   5   Remedial Teaching (Educational Support) 43
   6   Cultural Integration, Inclusiveness *(Ongoing Research)* 47
   7   Cooperation with Curative Schools *(Ongoing Research)* 51
   8   Teaching Mixed Age & Cross-Disciplinary Groups *(Ongoing Research)* 53
   9   Performance and Evaluation 57

Part 2
The Waldorf Curriculum Viewed "Horizontally" Grades 1–12 61

   1   Horizontal and Vertical Curriculum: A Comparison 63
   2   Background to Teaching in the Elementary-School Grades ... 65
   3   Horizontal Curriculum of the Elementary-School Years 75

      Transitional Classes 75
      Grades 1 – 3 76
      Grades 4 – 6 82
      Grades 7 – 8 89
4   Background to Teaching in the High-School Grades 99
5   Horizontal Curriculum of the High-School Years 107
      Grade 9 107
      Grade 10 113
      Grade 11 119
      Grade 12 125
Bibliography 135
Acknowledgements 141

PREFACE TO THE ENGLISH EDITION

This volume makes available in English a new and fully revised edition of a monumental description of the Waldorf curriculum (grades 1–12) undertaken by Tobias Richter at the behest of the International Forum for Waldorf/Steiner Education (formerly known as the Hague Circle). The first version of this comprehensive outline was initiated in the mid-1990s and has since been further expanded and updated. The fourth and most recent German edition of this work—under the title *Pädagogischer Auftrag und Unterrichtsziele: vom Lehrplan der Waldorfschule*—appeared in 2016 as a 700-page book accompanied by a multi-layered website (*www.lehrplan-waldorf.de*) rich in detailed suggestions and resources for curriculum studies.

As in the German version of the book, this latest English edition lays out the curriculum of the Waldorf school on two axes—"horizontally" year by year, "vertically" subject by subject. The first axis can be compared to the horizontal rungs of a ladder, wherein each grade is a rung viewed in terms of its major themes and goals for the year. The second axis can be compared to a collection of vertical flag poles—one for each academic, artistic, and practical subject—which one can shinny up from bottom to top in a single concentrated climb. In this sense, there are separate "flagpoles" for the banners of the language arts, mathematics, and the sciences; for the individual fine and performing arts; and for so-called practical activities such as technology and athletics. Like the row of flags fluttering outside the headquarters of the United Nations on the East Side of New York's Manhattan island, these subjects can be viewed separately or lined up, side by side.

Since the original editions of this encyclopedic work appeared first in German, it is to be expected that many of the examples offered along the way bear a Western European stamp. Likewise, references and footnotes guide the reader to German sources, including lectures by Rudolf Steiner not yet translated into English. Where appropriate, we offer English-language alternatives to suggested examples of the curriculum, as well as references to English versions of cited source materials or equivalent essays drawn from English-speaking authors.

The German edition, upon which this translation is based, contains three major sections. Parts I and II (representing about a quarter of the entire text) are reproduced here in full, but Part III—the "vertical" portion stretching to some 550 pages in the German version—will appear in English only online, as electronic subject-specific booklets mounted online (waldorf-resources.org/vertical-curriculum).

Over the years, many colleagues have worked intensely on the different versions of this book. In preparing this latest edition, Christian Boettger, Alexander Hassenstein, and Michael Zech from the Pedagogical Research Institute (Pädagogische Forschungsstelle) in Germany, as well as Claus-Peter Röh, Co-Leader of the Pedagogical Section of the School for Spiritual Science at the Goetheanum in Dornach, Switzerland, deserve special mention.

George Bernard Shaw is famously reputed to have observed that England and America are two nations divided by a common language. Perhaps in no discipline is this more the case than in education and the language of education. American readers will be familiar with references to the "language arts," which in other parts of the English-speaking world are referred to as the study of one's "native tongue;"

likewise, the Latin *practicum* is commonly used in American parlance, whereas elsewhere in the world one is more likely to speak of "extended field trips" or "practical studies." In short, then, we are opting for American terms and—in the spirit of colonial independence—American spellings.

Any publication concerning the content and themes of the Waldorf curriculum—like growing and maturing children it is intended to serve—must undergo continual revision and further development. Truly, then, this volume deserves the label "ongoing research," since it will always need to grow and be modified to meet the changing needs of current and future generations of children and adolescents.

At the same time, with the publication of this revised Waldorf curriculum, we offer readers a new connection to the original source that inspired it. Renewal arises afresh whenever one taps one's spiritual roots.

— Douglas Gerwin, Executive Director
Research Institute for Waldorf Education
Hudson, New York, June 2020

FOREWORD

"We should never fail to bear in mind that teaching involves a certain desire for complete freedom of action."[1]
— *Rudolf Steiner*

For some time now, the need for "something new" in the Waldorf world has been repeatedly voiced on all sides: *the new Waldorf teacher, the new Waldorf school...* And there are, of course, abundant reasons for expressing this need. It is, in fact, absolutely appropriate, for since 1919 Waldorf education has taken shape through the concrete actions of actual teachers in actual teaching situations in actual schools, proclaiming itself to be based upon the process of becoming —and thus meeting the New. How else can this be possible, except by constant renewal?

This question also applies to the Waldorf curriculum, especially in the case of a new edition like this one.

Although it follows a number of predecessors, this is a new form of curriculum. Following the *International Conference of the Waldorf School Movement,* the responsibility for this new edition was enthusiastically taken up, chiefly by the *Pädagogische Forschungsstelle*

---
1 Steiner (1990 *Practical Advice to Teachers,* GA 294)

beim Bund der Freien Waldorfschulen (the Pedagogical Research Institute of the Federation of Steiner/Waldorf Schools) in Stuttgart. They formed an editorial board, which sifted through each chapter and either undertook revisions or farmed them out to other writers and editors. This sifting process also revealed that certain contents or subjects are still widely assumed to be part of the curriculum, but in reality are no longer taught—for instance "classical languages" or the global term of "technology." In place of the latter subject and the practical topics suggested by Steiner, we now find the study of digital media and computer technology.

It was also felt to be important to incorporate new findings from the fields of educational and neurological research. Similarly, the intention was to include new research on the pedagogical effects of Waldorf methodological principles, as well as on the development of new lesson forms that open up the shifting of contextual emphasis. In connection with this latter field of interest, many areas that are either still under development and strongly subject to change, or that inhabit the margins of the curriculum, have been designated as *work in progress*. More thorough presentations of these areas can be found on the internet. The inclusion of contributions via an electronic medium gives immediate access to new and additional material as it becomes available, while at the same time making it possible to archive and maintain access to historical and traditional Waldorf material (such as, for instance, the above-mentioned subject of "technology"). As with the previous editions, what goes by the name of "the Waldorf curriculum" is in a continual state of development. This "work in progress" is the crucial factor, and none of the contributors had any notion of writing *the* definitive curriculum for the Waldorf school. Thus, the sub-title to this book *A Teacher's Guide to the Waldorf School Grades 1–12* means precisely what it says: an—not the—approach to the Waldorf school curriculum.

This approach unfolds in three parts:

- In the first part, the foundations of a Waldorf curriculum are described, including the anthroposophical view of human nature that provides a basis for curriculum design, and the special style of teaching and learning that is characteristic of a Waldorf school. In this edition, considerably more space has been given to this latter area.

- The second part contains an outline of the dynamics of child and adolescent development upon which the curriculum is built. The "horizontal" aspect of the curriculum, described year by year like rungs of a ladder, most clearly reveals this connection. Read as a musical score, it underlines the necessity of cooperation among all the colleagues teaching a particular class. In a Waldorf school, no teacher can be a soloist, because his or her actions are always directly related to the contributions of the others involved in the educational process.[2] Precisely because in the preparation and presentation of lessons the imagination and creativity of the teacher is essential, he or she stands in real danger of losing sight of the compositional whole. "Only when someone is hand-led beyond the arts [....] by a companion, friend, loving guide, does he fully take in the reality of mutual dependency. A form of education based upon training the authorial drive of the ego alone would lead to human alienation of a new and most painful kind." (Buber 1969, p. 17) An awareness of this mutual dependency and the development of the power of imagination are paramount motifs of Waldorf pedagogy. And if one of its main aims is to awaken and nurture social awareness and social action (Steiner 1984, p. 39), this applies to everyone. The horizontal curriculum offers ample opportunity for practising this "educational symphony" and turning it into an exemplary performance.

---

2 On various occasions Steiner pointed out the necessity for trans-disciplinary cooperation (Steiner 1990: GA 294, p. 47; Steiner 1975: GA 300c, pp. 182–190) and saw the teachers' meetings as ultimately the place where this would find its home, through exchange of practical experience and child discussions.

- Finally, the third part (to be made available in English only online) presents the curriculum "vertically," subject by subject: the structural description of all subjects from Grade 1 to Grade 12. Here, under "Principles and Aims," reference is made to the theoretical and phenomenological context within which the particular subject should be viewed, as described in Part II (included in this volume). Following that are considerations of what insights the subject offers in relation to the stages of development and what this means for classroom practice. Whatever comes to light as possible lesson content that relates to the principles and perspectives of the particular school year should be taken merely as an *example*. The actual children studying a particular subject are always the central focus (and not the other way around). The teacher is thus required to adapt the curriculum to the learners he or she is actually teaching.

Steiner's earliest ideas about creating a curriculum in tune with life already tended in this direction: "Future teachers must be capable of two things: studying the large-scale process of human development and observing the nature of the individual human being. Only equipped in this way will they be able to meet their true educational task: the integration of the individual into the rightly understood, overall developmental process of humanity, according to the particular endowments of the former." (Steiner 1989: GA 31, p. 624f.) The fulfilment of such a task requires on the part of the teacher both a thorough course of study and the schooling of his or her powers of perception. Steiner saw both as requirements for the teacher and merged them into a single piece of advice: to be able to perceive the expressions of a child's being and thus, by means of lesson content, to provide "developmental aid," the teacher must be engaged in self-education.

— *Christian Boettger, Alexander Hassenstein,*
Tobias Richter, Claus-Peter Röh, Michael Zech

ON THE PUBLICATION OF THIS GUIDE

"What should be taught should be derived only from knowledge of the developing individual and his or her aptitudes."[3]

— *Rudolf Steiner*

Rudolf Steiner's indications as to what a curriculum for the Waldorf school should contain were mostly given in lectures, and were never systematically organized by him, although he had intended to do this. Instead, this work was done by Caroline von Heydebrand shortly after Steiner's death, and was published in 1925 in a slim volume: *The Waldorf School Curriculum (Vom Lehrplan der freien Waldorschule)*. In this book, together with her colleagues, von Heydebrand collected Steiner's curricular suggestions, summarizing and systematizing them for parents and teachers. Thirty years later, in the form of an internally circulated typed manuscript, E. A. Karl Stockmeyer's work *Rudolf Steiner's Curriculum for the Waldorf Schools* appeared. This was a comprehensive collection of Steiner's utterances and writings on the

---

3 Steiner (1982): GA 24, p. 37

subject of pedagogy. The original title of this publication strongly implied that it was a set curriculum in the normal sense, and not a collection of sources on teaching method and content. For this reason, the title of the fourth edition was changed to *Rudolf Steiner's Indications for the Waldorf Curriculum*, since this wording more accurately reflected the book's intentions.

These bibliographical efforts by von Heydebrand and Stockmeyer studiously avoided anything programmatic or dogmatic – and yet they contributed to the establishment of a fixed canon of teaching content. What determines such content is that, in spite of all individual differences, it corresponds to a student's degree of maturity.

Caroline von Heydebrand described the special features of a Waldorf curriculum in the following terms: "The ideal curriculum would be one that would faithfully reflect the ever-changing picture of human nature in its various stages of development, but like every ideal it has to face the full reality of life and so must fit in with it. This reality has many facets: it involves the individuality of the teacher standing before a class; it involves the class itself, with the idiosyncrasies of every individual pupil; it involves the spirit of the times and the legal and administrative structures associated with the particular location of the school trying to put the curriculum into practice. All these circumstances modify the ideal curriculum, demanding changes and negotiations, and the educational task, which the nature of the growing child sets us, can be fulfilled only if the curriculum has the requisite flexibility and adaptability." (Heydebrand 1994, p. 11f)

In the course of the curricular debate that took place in the 1970's, the concise and pithy picture drawn by von Heydebrand was judged to be "too wishy-washy." Moreover, in numerous writings, Waldorf teachers were sharply criticized for often citing Steiner as a curricular authority in sources that could not be verified, because they were not generally available.

In 1992, the idea of compiling a general curricular framework was put forward by the "Hague Circle" (now *The International Forum for*

Steiner/Waldorf Education). This task was given to Tobias Richter, and a working group was chosen from the international Waldorf school movement with the instruction to take into account whatever existed in the way of curricular material worked out by various colleagues in particular schools.

The first draft in 1994 set off an extremely lively debate within the colleges of German Waldorf schools, in which both strong objections were expressed to the whole project or its particular form, as well as producing many stimulating, productive and helpful suggestions. Subsequently, these commentaries were all reviewed with the help of the Pädagogische Forschungsstelle beim Bund der freien Waldorfschulen and, where necessary, passed on for further consideration to new committees for specific subjects.

The manuscript edition that finally appeared in 1995 basically offered indications by means of examples, without seeking to be a definitively detailed, binding curriculum. It did, however, make clear what the anthroposophical conception of educating the whole human being had already produced, or was in process of developing, in the way of pedagogical practice.

Seven years later, the first version appeared in book form, considerably enlarged and thoroughly revised. It carried the same title as the present volume, which linked it to the curriculum of Caroline von Heydebrand—a deliberate gesture recognizing its predecessor.

It is important to mention that this work on the curriculum was taken up by Martyn Rawson in England, leading in the year 2000 to the valuable publication of *The Educational Tasks and Content of the Steiner Waldorf Curriculum*.

Besides the curriculum project initiated by the "Hague Circle," in 1996 the Pedagogical Section at the Goetheanum, in cooperation with the Pädagogische Forschungsstelle, also issued a curriculum, which appeared in a new edition in 2015. Its title—*Zur Unterrichtsgestaltung im 1. – 8. Schuljahr an Waldorf-/Rudolf Steiner Schulen (For Teaching in the 1st to 8th School Year at Waldorf- Rudolf SteinerSchools)*

– makes clear the intention lying behind this work. The intention was not to compile a comprehensive curriculum, but mainly to offer class teachers a helping hand.

In response to a call for a curriculum structured in terms of the teaching of skills, W. Götte, P. Loebell, and K.-M. Maurer took on this theme and in 2009 produced a thorough and comprehensive work: *Entwicklungsaufgaben und Kompetenzen. Zum Bildungsplan der Waldorfschule (Development Tasks and Competencies to the Waldorf School's Education Plan)*.

The short survey of publications described above does not include numerous curriculum booklets on specific subjects. Many such monographs have been published by the Pädagogische Forschungsstelle, and also in the series "Menschenkunde und Erziehung" by Verlag Freies Geistesleben and by the Verlag am Goetheanum (see also the internet bibliography under www.lehrplan-waldorf.de).

PART I

TASKS AND OBJECTIVES OF WALDORF EDUCATION

CHAPTER 1

THE FIRST WALDORF SCHOOL

"We should not ask: What knowledge and skills does the human being need in order to fit into the existing social order; rather: What lies in his or her nature, and how can it be developed? Only then will it be possible for the rising generation to continually infuse the social order with new impulses. Then, rather than each new generation being shaped to fit the existing society, the life of society will be whatever flows into it from these whole human beings."

— *Rudolf Steiner*

Waldorf education was developed by Rudolf Steiner in several stages. As early as 1888 we find him writing on the subject of school reform and sketching out fundamental principles for a future school system (Steiner 1966: GA 31, p. 624f.). From 1906 on he revisited these ideas in various lectures, giving them more concrete form; finally, in 1907, came the publication of *The Education of the Child in the Light of Anthroposophy* (Steiner 1987, GA 34).

Amidst the turmoil following the end of World War I, Steiner was asked to present his thoughts and ideas on cultural, economic, and social renewal. This he did in numerous lectures and publications (see e.g. Steiner 1976: GA 23). In this context, he recommended the emancipation of schools from the control of the state (school autonomy), and in bold strokes gave a sketch of an "all-in-one school" based on the laws of child development. These ideas were taken up by Emil Molt, the director of the Waldorf Astoria cigarette factory. His concern was not just to provide further education for his workers, but to create a school for their children as well. At his request, Steiner took on the conceptual development and leadership of the new school and gave it a broad pedagogical foundation. He summoned the initial circle of teachers and, over the next five years, worked together with them. In numerous lectures, seminars, school visits, and some seventy faculty meetings, the elements of Waldorf education and collegial self-administration took shape.

The "Free Waldorf School" opened in Stuttgart on 7 September 1919 as a "combined primary and high school," although the high school opened a year later. Right from the start, it was made available to children and parents from all social classes and was independent of any specific religious or philosophical orientation. With its 12 years of schooling for all children—the preschool program was added subsequently—it represented the very first comprehensive school in Germany.

This form of education led to the founding of further Waldorf or Rudolf Steiner schools in Germany and other countries. The National Socialists prohibited Waldorf education and eventually closed the schools in Germany, with the consequence that Waldorf education was practiced only in Great Britain, Switzerland, and the United States during the war years.[4] Immediately following the end of World War II in 1945, the reconstruction of the Waldorf movement began in Germany, and since then has expanded to include some 1,100 recognized Waldorf schools in over 60 countries worldwide.

---

4 The relationship of Waldorf education and anthroposophy to the National Socialists and their ideology has been examined by Uwe Werner in *Anthroposophy in the Time of Nazi Germany* 1933–1945, and by Wenzel M. Götte in *Erfahrungen mit Schulautonomie: Das Beispiel der Freien Waldorfschulen* (Stuttgart 2006).

CHAPTER 2

THE CURRICULUM IN ITS ANTHROPOSOPHICAL CONTEXT

"One of the most pernicious of errors is to assume that pedagogy is the science of the child—and not primarily the science of the human being."[5]

— *Janusz Korczak*

Rudolf Steiner developed a spiritual understanding of the human being known as anthroposophy, and Waldorf education is founded upon this form of knowledge, particularly its pedagogically relevant aspects. In laying the foundations of Waldorf education, Steiner coined special terms (for instance, the German word *Menschenkunde,* which in English can be rendered as "the study of the human being") that clearly reflect this anthroposophical background.

In his investigations on the nature of the human being, Steiner distinguished between three fundamental perspectives:

---

5 Korczak (1969): *Wie man ein Kind lieben soll.* Göttingen, p. 156

- that of the body, which is based on everything observable by the senses, and which views the human body in its relation to the mineral, plant, and animal kingdoms. This approach has much in common with the accepted scientific (and philosophical) view of human nature.

- that of the soul, which encompasses the world of feeling but also emphasises the forming of mental images and actions of the will. This approach includes a consideration of the organic bases of these activities, as well as an examination of how the soul organism (consisting of thinking, feeling, and will) develops over the course of a human biography. This requires a very broad, all-inclusive approach to psychology.

- finally, that of the spirit. This approach calls attention to what may be called the individuality, the core of the personality, the Self, or "I." This Self, as "spiritual essence," uses the body as its instrument and influences the life of the soul, but is also in turn influenced by them (cf. Leber 1989, p. 72).[6]

A further essential feature of the fundamentals of Waldorf education is the understanding of how the human soul and spirit are integrated into the human organism. From this perspective, three structural elements of the human organism can be identified (Steiner 1976: GA 21, p. 150–162):

- the first system incorporates the activity of the nerves and senses. It could be called the "head organism," after the organ where nerve and sense functions are centralized.

---

[6] Here we would like to point out a problem of terminology when used in conjunction with Steiner's special form of pedagogical anthropology. Steiner, and consequently all those who work in terms of his anthropology, uses concepts that carry a different connotation in contemporary psychology and educational theory. This is particularly apparent in connection with the above-mentioned "spiritual" perspective, insofar as it describes a non-material and non-emotional reality. (cf. Steiner 1995: GA 9, p. 48–51)

- the second structural element is the so-called "rhythmic system." It manifests in the rhythmical processes of the human organism, especially in respiration and blood circulation.
- the third system is a combination of all the organs and activities directly involved in metabolism and reproduction, along with the limbs.

The anthroposophical view of the human being has provided the framework for numerous scientific studies (see Rittelmeyer 2002), and, in turn, is constantly absorbing new findings from many different fields of modern research (human biology, medicine, psychology, etc.) (Kranich 1998, 2003). Thus it possesses a high degree of scientific relevance. However, to equate it with the anthropological basis of mainstream educational theory is to sell it rather short, since Steiner's pedagogical anthropology—namely the anthroposophical view of the human being—is intended to be something more: it is a way of providing teachers with a schooling of their cognitive and emotional life profound enough to enable them to cultivate empathy. Here empathy is considered as a comprehensive form of knowledge that grants the teacher intuitive insight into the child's basic spiritual needs; these include related questions, thoughts, feelings, and motives as well as the child's general well-being and state of health (Steiner 1961, GA 36, p. 288f.; Kiersch 2010).

Steiner's hope was that the teacher's encounter with the anthroposophical description of human nature would inform the teacher's ability to structure the curriculum in a dynamically responsive, individual way: "The child becomes the book wherein the teacher may read what best to do. Thus we develop a fine sense for what should happen with the child, for example, at a particular moment. One such moment is the one that occurs between the ages of nine and ten." (Steiner 1979: GA 304a, p. 117)

Learning to "read" children in this way demands at the very least—and Steiner repeatedly makes mention of this—a detailed study of the constitution of body, soul, and spirit, as well as their interrelationships. Only on this basis is it possible to observe the working of the Self within the physical, psychological, and spiritual processes of each young person. The goal of education in the broadest sense is to accompany young people through these challenges so that they develop self-determination and personal autonomy, while at the same time becoming aware of their social responsibilities (cf. Leber 1993: p. 154ff.).

From this view of the nature of education arise all considerations of teaching methodology. Likewise, lesson content—always rooted in the developmental stage typical of the child's age, as well as his or her personal situation—has the character of an "instrument," a pedagogical tool.

This, however, does not imply that command of lesson content is of secondary importance, or can ever be disregarded. It is only through the teacher's intense study and personal involvement with teaching material that it can ever have the desired effect. Thus, Waldorf teachers conceive of their teaching as a pedagogical opportunity to cultivate the young person's cognitive, aesthetic, and practical abilities. The curriculum as a whole must reflect this. Accordingly, it contains the full range of subjects: the cognitively oriented, the artistic, and the craft-based and practical. In addition to this arrangement, however, emphasis is placed on the need to structure each particular learning process holistically. This means that every topic in a particular subject area has the potential to be thematically enlarged upon by other subjects. Holistic also means that the two complementary modes of thinking (the analytic and the synthetic) are regularly practiced or, more accurately, it means that both are incorporated into the learning process in keeping with the basic human need for rhythm. More will be said about this later.

In the context of a holistic approach to education, mention must be made of another realm Steiner regarded as crucial for the overall formation of character: namely, the religious realm, which always comes into play when young persons seek insight into the secrets of the world. Thus, Waldorf education has an inherently ethical-religious dimension. Actual religion lessons can, indeed should, be given by representatives of the various religious communities and denominations, in classes selected according to the wishes of parents or of students at an appropriate age. Alternatively, the teachers themselves may offer non- or transdenominational classes—the so-called "free religion lessons."

A child-centered, developmentally based curriculum, as presented here, can serve only as an orientational framework, offering the teacher the possibility of freely—and, of course, responsibly—selecting lesson content to meet the needs of a particular teaching situation.

In this connection the principle of teaching by means of "the symptomatic example" is of decisive importance. To meet the challenges of the moment, but without losing track of the educational intention, the teacher will sometimes replace old content with new, or purposefully leave something out. In short, the teacher must have the courage to choose according to the pedagogical demands of the moment. Holding doggedly to fixed or prescribed content—thereby jeopardizing the children's willingness to learn, their joy in knowledge and discovery, their curiosity and wonder—must be avoided at all costs.

Young people, in developing their faculty of judgment, seek answers to issues of the times and to questions concerning their own personal lives. Thus, it is essential that the curriculum take this yearning into account. This was one of Steiner's firm intentions for the Waldorf school from the time of its inception. For instance, in speaking of what should be "on the program," he stated that "all teaching must promote learning about the practicalities of life."[7] (Steiner 1964: GA 192, p. 98) Questions about technology in the widest sense should not be confined to the context of one subject, but should be taken

---

7 Here Steiner used the word *Lebenskunde*, by which he meant the social and educational implications of a range of topics having to do with practical life: e.g., farming, various forms of technology, commercial activities, trade, branches of industry, etc.

up and handled in an age-appropriate way wherever they arise (cf. Steiner 1990: GA 294, 168ff.).

The same goes for potentially controversial areas of contemporary life, such as ecology, migration, IT, media, health and substance abuse, terrorism, etc., as well as issues around sexuality. (On these topics, see the relevant pages on the internet at www.lehrplan-waldorf.de or waldorf-resources.org/vertical-curriculum).

Steiner refers to a further important developmental aspect of Waldorf education when he speaks of the forming of living concepts "which can change in the course of the child's later life," instead of giving endlessly repeated definitions. The former are distinguished from the latter in that their growth ideally take place "organically" in other words, through an inner process of differentiation. Steiner describes this process as "analytic." In terms of method, it is reflected in the principle of beginning with the whole and then proceeding to consideration or investigation of the parts (the details), though always in relation to the whole. This is exemplified in the way subjects such as writing, arithmetic, language arts (or what in Britain is called home-language), history, and geography are introduced, and descriptions may be read in the relevant sections. The suggestions made there should be viewed in the context of a three-step method, the main features of which are as follows: First the problem should be presented as comprehensively as possible, before beginning to analyze it, encouraging the learners to tease out the details. Then in a third phase—the synthetic—a (provisional) concept is formed out of the results of the analytical process.

For Steiner, the whole point of this way of working lies in its awakening effect. This is an expression of one of the essential aims of Waldorf education: "Basically, the intention behind what we do in the Waldorf school is not to educate, but to awaken. For everything nowadays is about awakening." (Steiner 1988: GA 217, p. 36) A method of forming concepts so that they are inherently alive, capable of growth and "enlightening," ultimately paves the way for education toward autonomy and self-determination—in short, education toward freedom: "From the soul's perspective all our actions are based upon an analytical activity, the effect of which is that in the life of our normal waking consciousness we are able to develop freedom." (Steiner 1991: GA 301, p. 153)

All this implies that what has been planted as "seeds," or experienced at a certain time, will ripen and mature later, for the long-term effects of the curricular elements currently being taught must always be taken into account. Thus, the teaching material must provide the stimulus for individual lifelong learning, fostering a desire to learn and engage in research, creativity, and social responsibility.

Finally, given that we are speaking of a curriculum linked to the process of development, it needs to be viewed in its wider social and political context. Internationally, the curriculum is faced with having to meet the needs of a wide variety of historical, political, social, and cultural realities. It is therefore possible for schools to keep to the same educational principles while adjusting lesson content in relation to linguistic, literary, historical, sociological, geographical, and economic conditions in their respective countries.

CHAPTER 3

ADMINISTRATION THROUGH COMMUNITY PARTICIPATION

"Changing things doesn't necessarily make them better, but if we want them to be good, they have to change."[8]

— *Georg Christoph Lichtenberg*

The founding of the first Waldorf school in September 1919 is closely related to social initiatives and ideas that took shape amid the upheavals at the end of World War I. Since 1917, Steiner had been working on the idea of a threefold ordering of the social organism; out of this comprehensive vision of social organization had come the insight that a form of education seeking to ground itself uncompromisingly upon human freedom and individuality should itself be free from external control. In its organization, and above all in its curriculum, it needed to be free from the cultural dictates of a hierarchical, administrative bureaucracy.

"To be able to work properly as an educator one must be in a position to face the recipients of education in a free and independent fashion. The guidelines for one's actions must depend upon *knowledge* of

---

8 Lichtenberg (1984): *Sudelbücher,* p.470, Munich.

human nature, of the organization of society and so on, but not upon *regulations or laws* imposed from outside [....] From such independent members of the social organism will come individuals willing and eager to engage in society." (Steiner 1982: GA 24, p.39)

On the eve of the pedagogical training course that he had convened in Stuttgart, Steiner solemnly spelled out the task of the teachers assembled before him: "The Waldorf school must be a real cultural deed, a deed that will renew the spiritual life of our times [....] The success of this cultural deed is given into your hands [....] Everyone must engage wholly right from the start. For this reason we will set up this school in terms not of governance, but of administration, and this administration will be run on republican lines. In a true teachers' republic we will not be cushioned by edicts from a headmaster, rather we must find in ourselves that which bestows upon us the possibility of taking full responsibility for whatever we have to do. Everyone must share this responsibility." (Steiner 1992 GA 293, p. 13ff.) On another occasion, in the context of his activities in support of the threefold social organism, he emphatically declared: "The administration of educational establishments, the implementation of courses of study and educational aims should only be in the hands of people who *are also involved* in teaching, or otherwise productively engaged in cultural life. Such people would divide their time between teaching, or other culturally creative activity, and administration of the education system." (Steiner 1982: GA 24, p. 41f.) These forceful statements place every college of teachers in the position of having to work out an interpretation of them, and thus find a way of realising Steiner's standards.

In the years immediately following the founding of the first Waldorf school, it was natural for Steiner to take on pedagogical leadership and personnel management. The minutes of the college meetings show this in action (Lindenberg 1997, p. 676ff.). The collegial self-administration that he initiated came fully into play only after he became ill; schools subsequently founded put these principles into practice in widely differing ways. Increasingly (from 1946 onward), parents also became involved in taking on organizational responsibility. Here school self-administration does not just mean working out formal rules for parental representation and voting rights, but also establishing and practicing managerial participation and co-responsibility. For several decades now, both state and independent schools have been putting various forms of participation into practice, some also involving high-school students. Thus, the modern school sees itself as a community of parents (or guardians), teachers, and students. According to the level of responsibility assigned to each of these three groups, all have the duty and the right to be involved in decision-making. In many countries, in accordance with the regulations for private schools, some "spokesperson" will be named by the college as their "head." This person is responsible for external relations, especially orchestrating administrative cooperation with the education authorities, but this need not compromise the internal autonomy and community integrity of the pedagogical and administrative running of the school.

Waldorf schools nowadays are run as non-profit organizations, cooperatives, or limited companies, and the form they take is often determined by the parent body. A school normally opts for a particular type of organization at the time of its founding. Whoever is constituted as the legal entity—for example, the board of the school association—is responsible for all legal and financial matters in close consultation with the college, which is in turn solely responsible for what happens in the school's classrooms.

The founding of a Waldorf school usually arises from the commitment and enthusiasm of a group of parents and/or teachers, often assisted and supported by a local mentor or an advisor provided by the International Forum. By now quite a body of experience has been built up around questions of changing a school's form of organization. Usually this happens either as a result of changes in the law or because it is the will of the community.

For teachers, students, and parents (or guardians) alike, it is a testing ground for social competence, an opportunity to learn what it means to shape and be responsible for a whole community. Because the life of the school flows from the initiative and commitment of all those involved in it, they are the only ones who can manage it.

In recent decades, quite a number of schools have made efforts to professionalize their organizational development to create a clear and effective administrative structure and to prevent conflicts and teacher overload. Working together in such a process usually leads those involved to intensify their identification with the school, and brings a new awareness of the range of responsibilities of both teachers and parents. The sense of personal responsibility is indeed encouraged by such involvement in the self-administration of a school, because in all decision-making—even in group decisions—the individual is fundamental. In such a context, a crisis exposes the fact that everyone involved needs to change. Self-administration, in other words, schools individual community awareness. This form of governance does not exist as an end in itself, nor as an opportunity for self-realization for those concerned, but rather to ensure that the educational needs of teachers and students are humanely and responsibly met.

Besides what has just been described, the school community has ample opportunity for developing other forms of participation and cooperation. Among these are school festivals, courses, exhibitions, lectures, concerts, and, above all, adult education workshops, which can also be open to the public. "Open partnership between teachers and parents is an essential prerequisite of a school's continued existence" (Dietz 2006, p. 140). It is imperative that Waldorf parents know and understand the intentions behind the educational principles being used in their children's school. Only when the parents have this specific pedagogical insight, and the teachers get to know them, is there a basis upon which they can be cooperatively responsible for carrying the school.

The various vehicles of this educational cooperation between parents (or guardians) and school include the following:

Parent evenings: At parent meetings of a particular class, the teacher can characterize the pedagogical and developmental stage the students have reached. Descriptions of what is being done in various subject areas, and why, help the parents feel involved in the life of the school and in their children's development.

Home visits and parent interviews: Pedagogical problems arising with specific students, as well as questions parents might have, can be discussed with the relevant teacher either in the course of a home visit or in a private meeting.

General parent evenings and parent meetings: In lectures and conversations initiated by the college of teachers and/or the board of trustees and/or (parent) committees, questions of general educational interest and problems affecting school life as a whole can be discussed.

Festivals,[9] lectures, concerts, exhibitions, seminars: These kinds of events forge and deepen contacts within the school community and with the public at large. Courses in arts and crafts, as well as pedagogical study groups, provide parents and other interested parties with the opportunity to expand their knowledge and practical experience, and also gain insight into the methods and aims of a Waldorf school.

The class community is based on the children's collective experience of what they learn in their lessons, led and accompanied by their teachers. But it is not just a forum for the successful presentation of educational content: It is a living community, where all kinds of questions can be aired and discussed—personal motivation, current world affairs, or local issues such as school rules and discipline.

The students, especially in the upper grades, should become aware that they also carry some responsibility for the school as a whole. In

---

[9] These can either be seasonal, whole-school festivals, or gatherings to mark the end of a month or a term. At the latter, the ongoing work of the various classes is shared in some way. Thus, the students have a chance to experience what their peers in other classes are doing and also get to know them. Some of these festivals may be open to the public.

many Waldorf schools there is a functioning auxiliary student administration (student council), which identifies and articulates student issues, but which may also deal with matters of more general school interest. The student representatives also organise their own regional, national, and international events.

Another salient feature of a Waldorf school is the close cooperative interaction among the teachers. The weekly teachers' meeting serves the purpose of facilitating general pedagogical study, furnishing research material in particular subject areas and methodology, and providing further training for teachers; in addition, it promotes the exchange of information, advice, and mutual support. It considers and decides all educational and administrative matters. Weighty decisions are made in consultation with the school board. A committee or mandate group takes care of details like the preparation of the meeting agenda and the decision-making process. Parent representatives from each class also meet regularly, and visitors from among the teachers or student body often participate in their deliberations.

An important body that could or should be a feature of all schools is a "mediation committee." Whatever its name, it can convene when conflicts arise and take whatever action is necessary to alleviate them.

Experience shows that, in a school that is practicing self-administration, there are so many tasks to be managed that every teacher—varying from year to year—needs to take on at least one of them.

CHAPTER 4

TEACHING AND LEARNING PROCESSES

"What we call invention or discovery in a higher sense is the concerted activation of an original feeling for truth, long since formed in secret, that leads in a flash to some fruitful insight. It is an inner revelation, arising from our reading of the outer world, that gives us an intimation of our kinship with the divine. It is a synthesis of world and spirit, bestowing blessed assurance of the eternal harmony of existence."[10]

— *Johann Wolfgang Goethe*

LEARNING PROCESSES
Learning as a Rhythmic Process

The design of a curriculum and class schedule, or timetable, as well as the choice of subjects, attempts to reflect the *rhythmic course* of the school year, week, and day, and to take into account the natural

---
10 Goethe (1977): *Naturwissenschaftliche Schriften – Aphorismen und Fragmente.* In: *Sämtliche Werke*, Zürich, p. 752.

alternation of rest, attentive receptivity, and the need for movement. As far as possible the theoretical, artistic, and practical subjects in the schedule/timetable will be ordered with such an alternation in mind, providing breaks that serve as transitions between the processing and further acquisition of teaching content. Thus, the methodology of teaching and learning, starting from a relationship to the real world, builds upon the sequence of the three qualitative levels of any learning process: namely, apprehension, understanding, and command of the material:

1 Perception, experience, observation, experiment

2 Recall, description, characterization, recording

3 Processing, analysis, abstraction, generalization, deepening: determination of connections and lawful regularities, concept formation

Here, of course, it is important to realize that we cannot expect to reach the third phase of this process in one lesson. After experience (1) and description (2) there will be a gap, long enough to include the night; by this means, a certain detachment from the lesson content is made possible. Not until the following day will the final step in the learning process be completed. In this way Waldorf education attempts to work with the polarities active in human development; for if we are to focus on developing not just cognitive abilities but the abilities of the whole person, we must take into account the dynamics of learning and forgetting, the conscious and the unconscious, waking and sleeping. (cf. Wiehl 2015, p. 224f.)

Learning as a Holistic Process

It is Waldorf education's intention to engage the whole person in the process of learning, and this can be met through creative repetition, artistic and practical consolidation of whatever has been learned in the way described above. This method of learning, of course, also reflects Steiner's stated pedagogical aim of awakening young people's sense of freedom and sending them forth in this spirit. It is only after the full complement of the senses has been engaged and the topic in hand has become a specific experience that the process of forming a judgment should be undertaken, for "every judgement that is not based upon a rich store of valued personal experience creates obstacles in the path of the person making it." (Steiner 1987: GA 34, p. 342) Essentially, the learning process and its outcome are the same thing. For the student, this opens up the possibility of being involved in an inductive or phenomenological approach to the lesson, unencumbered by pre-formulated theories, that permits his or her own experience to form the basis of knowledge. "Only through action based on knowledge can freedom be realised." (Schneider 1982: p. 179)

This also implies that the general headings in science textbooks do not determine the choice of teaching content. Rather, the teacher is called upon to find suitable material for each stage of a child's development and to present a carefully tailored selection as specifically and creatively as possible. The upshot of this approach is that teaching and learning occur only through direct, creative interaction between teacher and student.

Learning as an Individual Process

The three universal levels of the learning process described above are also highly relevant in relation to individual learning, since students are involved in the discovery of knowledge in a variety of complementary ways: first, through outer and inner activity in the gathering of their own experience, and second, through an unconscious inner activity that follows when an interval of the night is inserted between the gathering of experience and the formation of concept or theory. During this period of latency, self-generated insights ripen, which often means that the next day, knowledge is only a small step away.

The students thus experience knowledge as something that grows of itself, and that the path leading to it from experience is a continuum. Steiner's conviction was that in such a way students would arrive at an individual understanding deep and secure enough to enable them to take personal responsibility for their words and actions.

Equally universal as Steiner's pedagogical principles—and compatible with Waldorf education—are the ideas of Martin Wagenschein (cf. Wagenschein 1968), who, on the one hand, places experience at the beginning of all learning, and, on the other, emphatically appeals to the student's individual responsibility in the process of learning. Wagenschein outlines the stages of his didactic path in terms of a trio of concepts: exemplary, genetic, and Socratic.

The exemplary stage entails breaking down the range of possible teaching materials into a set of essential topics, selected so that they provide students with the opportunity for key sensory and intellectual experiences. This is based on the conviction that if learning is to last, it must always involve the student in direct, personal engagement with the phenomenon in question. Teaching in this sense is not about covering as much material as possible, but about satisfying the students' natural eagerness to learn. The criterion for the selection of teaching topics is that they should include more than just one area of the discipline concerned. More important, however, is that the topics chosen serve as a mirror of the discipline as a whole. As Wagenschein puts it: "The study of exemplars is the opposite of specialization. Its intention is not to single out the parts, but in the part to find the whole. 'Impossible'? – certainly, if all you can do is add." (Wagenschein 1968: p. 32)

The genetic stage means, again in Wagenschein's words, "exploration into the unknown," rather than "viewing clearly identified specimens in a museum" (Wagenschein 1968: p. 69). This is also a fundamental feature of original science. Teaching undergoes a change of perspective, away from the result, toward the original question. To begin with an exemplary phenomenon evokes questions in the student, and these in turn determine the next step in the lesson. Thus, the lesson becomes a search for answers, and the students themselves are the agents of this process. In consequence, answers may lead to new questions, or even down the wrong path. Wagenschein assigns considerable pedagogical potential to mistakes: "Expository teaching fears nothing more than doubt and error: thus it not only denies itself the possibility of productive ambiguity, but it also fails to achieve that certainty which, having overcome it, is proof against all confusion. In real science things are no different." (Wagenschein 1968: p. 69)

The Socratic stage changes the teacher's role from the one who has answers to the one who has questions, thus avoiding outcomes-oriented teaching. Things are held in a state of suspension; space is kept open for the students to take up the role of authentic researchers. According to the circumstances in the class, the teacher, as in a Socratic dialogue, can use the question to advance the discussion, stall it, or create uncertainty, which can be important for students who are too quick to leap to conclusions. The essential thing is that the students are constantly encouraged to think for themselves. An observation by Georg Christoph Lichtenberg points to the long-term effects of such a pedagogical principle: "That which one has to discover for oneself leaves a pathway in the mind, which can later be used for some other purpose." (Lichtenberg 1958: p. 141).

THE TEACHER AND THE LEARNING PROCESS

In Waldorf education teaching and learning are seen not as a purely intellectual exercise, but as an activity that encompasses the full range of human faculties. The preparation of any kind of teaching material is the first step in the transformational process, since it is geared toward the actual developmental phase of a certain age group. The next steps in the transformation then occur through the activity of assimilating the material—an experiential process from which knowledge emerges in conceptual form.

These processes of creative responsiveness and transformation are characteristic of the way artists work with their material. This is why Steiner was inclined to designate pedagogical practice as *the art of education* (Steiner 1979: GA 304a, p. 119). He was always trying to challenge the teacher to become an (educational) artist (Steiner 1993: GA 302a, p. 18), someone whose whole heart and soul is engaged in the pedagogical performance, and who together with the students is constantly forging fresh encounters with aspects of the world. Art here does not refer to a particular subject, but—in Schiller's sense of the word (cf. Schiller 2000)—to the active process of creating knowledge. The human being imbues his or her desire for knowledge with a love of it, just like an artist at work or someone experiencing a piece of art and inwardly recreating it.

The class teacher and the subject teacher

The class teacher is a profession specific to Waldorf schools, with no direct equivalent in any other educational system. The anthroposophical concept of education finds living expression in the practice of being a class teacher, a profession that is predicated upon an active process of comprehensive self-development.

Learning during the school years is a complex process, continually unfolding year by year. The Waldorf view is that learning cannot attain its proper intensity unless it occurs in a stable context built on relationships of trust and concern for personal well-being. For students, a central person they can depend upon is the prerequisite for their success in learning. In a Waldorf school this person is the class teacher. The fact that, both in preparing subject matter and in the act of teaching it, he or she is constantly learning, is a fundamental motivational principle in Waldorf education. In developing a firm grasp of whatever topic he or she wishes to bring to the students, the class teacher sets a powerful example. Assuming that a class teacher stays with the same class for eight years, the palette of subjects includes language arts, arithmetic, practical skills, geography, history, nature study, physics, chemistry, drawing, and painting. Apart from all this, a class teacher also needs to be a reasonably competent musician and an accomplished storyteller.

Prerequisite to learning is self-motivation on the part of each student, and, of course, self-activation on the part of the teacher is also indispensable for the learning process. Pedagogically speaking, specialized knowledge acquired through academic study or professional training is of less value than, on the one hand, a constantly exercized will to learn, and, on the other, a readiness to venture into new subjects with interest and openness. This means both the teacher's self-learning and his or her self-education—the effort to develop those faculties that help toward a more comprehensive understanding of the child. This attitude of the teacher is a decisive factor in creating a positive climate of learning in the classroom.

Only someone who demonstrates a child-like willingness to learn and a keen interest in knowing all about the world can truly animate these same processes in the children. To be able to grow with the students in their emotional and cognitive development as they pass through the elementary grades in itself justifies the existence of the Waldorf class teacher.

The effect of the teaching material on the class teacher, and the associated changes that it brings about in him or her, are in turn decisively important in promoting learning in the child. In teaching arithmetic, for instance, the class teacher is a different kind of person than when teaching grammar; geography contrasts with history in a similar way. In having direct experience of this living model, the child has the opportunity of learning just how capable of change the human being can be.

The basic intention of the curriculum is that it should be pedagogically effective in two important ways: by matching the teaching material to the age group, and by highlighting its many cross-disciplinary relationships. Since the curriculum is not an abstract, prescriptive document—as has already been mentioned—it can arise anew within the specific social context of every lesson through the creativity of the class teacher. The system by which the class teacher is responsible for all main lesson subjects over many years is a good way of achieving this intention. The class teacher designs his or her lesson content based on direct familiarity with each individual child and with the group dynamics of the class, and thus is in a position to know how best to develop the students' abilities.

In a Waldorf school, the work of subject teachers also has its pedagogical basis in their ability to be personally in tune with the students' development and to build up a relationship of trust with them. In addition, what counts is the teacher's ability to represent or embody a particular subject: a foreign language teacher should see him- or herself as a representative of a certain language region; a music teacher represents life's musical aspects, etc. Here, also, beyond the universality of the class teacher, what comes to the fore is the specialized command of a particular subject. This quality applies in the high school as well, where all main lesson blocks are taught by experts in their subject. This subject orientation creates a new way of meeting the world and of forming judgments.

The children's learning and development are enhanced when they feel that their class teachers and subject teachers are working together. A school divided into class teachers, on the one hand, and subject teachers, on the other, into main lesson versus special subjects, would be contrary to all intentions. The foundation of cooperation is, among other things, regular class meetings in which all those who teach a particular class get together to discuss issues arising out of their work with the students. Class teachers and subject teachers sitting in on each other's lessons and taking joint responsibility for the administrative organization of a class are further ways to achieve a climate of mutual trust and cooperation.

TEACHING STRUCTURES AND METHODS

Students in a Waldorf school participate in virtually all of the curriculum since it arises from the general characteristics of various phases of development. A special feature of the Waldorf school is that, with very few exceptions, there is no curricular differentiation according to gender. Subjects such as handwork, needlework, gardening, crafts, and technology are studied by both boys and girls. Many subjects do indeed involve divisions, but never according to gender or ability. Differentiation according to ability can be envisaged in the case of foreign language teaching, as Steiner suggested (Steiner 1975: GA 300b).

Depending on their particular nature, subjects are taught either as main lessons or as special subject lessons. The former are given in *blocks or modules*, the latter in recurring *track or run-through lessons*. Theoretical, artistic, and practical subjects that lend themselves to concentrated study of a few weeks are offered in the form of *main lesson blocks*. Other subjects, particularly skills that require constant *practice*, are done as year-long *track/run-through lessons*.

Main lesson blocks: This didactic form, originally introduced by Steiner, is a way of economizing the teaching by concentrating course material, while at the same time paving the way for cross-disciplinary teaching. (Steiner 1990: GA 295). Over a period of several weeks, in a so-called *main lesson*[11] of about 110 minutes every day, specific aspects of a particular subject will be worked on by a particular class. This learning rhythm enhances the retention of what has been learned and supports the development of abilities. When a main lesson block ends, detachment from its content—"productive forgetting," it has been called—naturally occurs. This is followed, when the next block on the subject starts at some later time, by a review of what was

---

11 This daily focus—every morning for several weeks—upon a developmentally attuned theme creates continuity, as well as the possibility of crossing disciplinary boundaries. The designation *main lesson* refers to this centering upon a main theme, not to the teaching of a "main subject" as opposed to a (by implication less important) "subsidiary subject."

previously learned. These are important processes in the psychology of learning, as shown not only by neurological research, but especially by chronobiological research (cf. Rosslenbroich 1994; Schad 1991, p. 90). Keen attention must be paid to arranging main lesson time so that it involves a rich and carefully structured variety of activities, for otherwise fatigue rather than concentration sets in. Often the teacher will plan various phases in the lesson, or at least consciously vary his or her teaching methods. Subjects typically taught in main lesson format include language arts (sometimes called home languages), mathematics/geometry, geography/economics, history/social studies, biology, physics, chemistry, art history.

Track/run-through lessons: Music, eurythmy, art, foreign languages, handwork, crafts, gymnastics are all examples of subjects usually taught in recurring track/run-through classes (whether as single or double periods). However, as soon as the work attains a certain level, these lessons can take on a block form as a main lesson. Language or "home language" and mathematics, in addition to being taught as main lessons, are also taught as run-through lessons. Here also attempts are constantly being made to economise by bundling the regular track classes into several blocks spread over the year, thus transforming these subjects into additional main lessons. However, a subject like mathematics, which like foreign (sometimes called "world") languages depends on regular practice, can be taught as main lessons only if the blocks are spread over the year in a regular sequence.

Special projects and field trips: In Waldorf schools, a basic concern right from the start is that students be presented with material that addresses and challenges the whole person. As a rule, special projects are designed to forge links to a central theme. This applies to projects like puppet or marionette shows, as well as other kinds of theater projects, or social service projects in the local community involving care and support for others. Field trips, especially in the upper elementary and high school years, allow students to experience the world beyond the confines of the classroom. Especially in areas such as science and technology, but also in the arts (visits to museums or exhibitions), day-long field trips or museum visits make concrete what has been covered more theoretically at school.

Practicums and field trips: Waldorf schools set great store by these specially organized excursions, which begin in the upper elementary school and carry on through high school. As a rule they last from two to three weeks (though sometimes considerably longer), giving students a chance to engage fully in a project, and with the people involved. The challenges built into these practicums and field-trips are geared toward particular phases of development and vary from school to school. As far as possible, the goal is for students not just to observe but to participate in actual work. Connections with the natural world and with processes of food production are made possible by forestry, agricultural, and ecological field trips. Experience of the world of work comes through practicums in craft workshops and industrial plants, while social practicums provide students with the opportunity to do community service through placements in nursing homes, children's homes, and social service organizations. The land-surveying field trip in grade 10 plays a special role, in that it involves the practical application of mathematical skills learned in the classroom. For young people, besides the academic and physical challenges, there is always a strong element of social challenge in these practicums, especially if they take place in an unfamiliar setting, or even abroad. Such ventures are prepared and reviewed by the class as a whole, together with the relevant teachers, and their experiences are then presented afterwards in the form of a report, sometimes before the whole school. Documentation takes the form of journals, notebooks, or portfolios. Depending on the pedagogical aim of the practicum, it might also be carried out by the whole class together, or in small groups.

All practical and artistic subjects have exacting requirements. Class sizes and teaching methods must correspond to the space and equipment available, so that each individual's work can receive appropriate attention.

Of course, the question of the method or form in which academic material should be presented, practiced, and assimilated also applies to the more theoretical subjects. Waldorf education always bases its teaching methodology on the behavior and development of the students (cf. Steiner 1979: GA 304a). In addition, it should always promote individual learning in the context of the class as a whole. Some of the teaching structures and methods most frequently practiced in Waldorf schools include:[12, 13]

- ***Integrated teaching*** (Gudjons 2011, p. 25), in which the teacher introduces a particular theme to the whole class as a way of motivating further individual work that goes more deeply into the subject. This approach can lead, for instance, to the formation of various learning groups; similarly, the further course of the main lesson can be developed and structured in dialogue with the students. Here, too, a high priority is placed on the nurturing of social awareness. In combination with a focus on individual learning, a climate of trust develops, forming a secure foundation for the learning process as a whole. A further element in this way of working is the possibility of incorporating various arts into the developing structure, if they serve the aesthetic purpose of reflecting, complementing, and deepening the main theme. The composition of this kind of lesson requires much variation of method, so a rich diversity of elements can unfold.

- ***Group teaching,*** in situations where an overall theme naturally divides into a series of sub-themes, resulting in different groups doing different tasks. Clear formulation of the tasks is essential here, so that all students know exactly what is required

---

[12] See footnote 11

[13] Detailed descriptions of these options can be found in books published by Waldorf Publications and SteinerBooks or on the internet at the Online Waldorf Library (www.waldorflibrary.org) of the Research Institute for Waldorf Education (RIWE).

of them. Since Waldorf schools are made up of mixed ability classes, work in small groups offers an excellent opportunity for creative social interaction. In addition to a heightened level of engagement with the lesson content, the dynamic group processes that arise are of great value in building social awareness and self-confidence. Moreover, since the effectiveness of Waldorf education relies not only on the "what" of the curriculum content but ever more on the "how," this method attains a high degree of importance.

- *The flexible or movable classroom* (Bochum model), which takes into account the urge—especially among young children—to move and the necessity to provide for their basic physical development through an increased range of sensory-motor learning experiences. That there is an evident relationship between human learning and movement is borne out by research in neurobiology and developmental psychology (cf. Beer/Schwarz 2012). This approach attempts to support this need by viewing the classroom as an open space and equipping it with movable furniture that can be used in a variety of ways. Thus a whole host of different possibilities for interaction arises: besides supporting specific movements and exercises, this setup promotes development of the children's social skills and self-motivation (cf. Carle 2014). The use of the movable classroom may require the re-organization of the whole (primary school) schedule/timetable; to be able to respond to the pedagogical needs of the moment, teachers practicing this method may be inclined to view the school morning as a whole, with special subject lessons and break or recess time inserted at flexible times.

All the lesson structures described above are aimed at encouraging self-motivated learning. As with the lesson content, there can be no question of a prescribed set of methods, for the conditions under which education occurs are diverse and always changing.

What never changes is the view of the child as a human being steadfastly on the path to self-discovery. "I will only be truly educating the human being when I do nothing to interfere with his or her Self, but rather wait until this Self is itself capable of taking hold of what I as a teacher have placed at its disposal. And so I follow the child's growth toward that moment when I can say: now the Self, in the fullness of its freedom, has been born; I have only provided the groundwork for its becoming aware of itself." (Steiner 1986: GA 308)

As a corollary to this central motif, the role of individuality and self-motivation in the learning process may arise. The following methodological approaches are intended to provide opportunities for individuality and self-motivation:

- educational opportunities that grant students the space and time to develop their own ideas and projects and require them to be responsible for their implementation. Classic examples of these are the year-long Grade 12 and Grade 8 projects;

- methods of documenting learning processes, such as the portfolio, in which students reflect on the steps they have taken and envisage those they will take in the future, thereby assuming responsibility for directing their own educational path;

- elective classes that give students the opportunity to supplement the curriculum by following their own talents or inclinations, thereby becoming partially involved in creating their own educational path;

- use of the Goethean (phenomenological) method of scientific observation, in which one characterizes a phenomenon by collecting and organizing observations (cf. Finke 2016), assuming the student is familiar with the method and can be left to design and carry out the process;

- the Wagenschein method, with the schooling of independent thinking as a basis for any kind of self-motivated learning.

TEACHING MATERIALS

"Passive" materials: Standard textbooks, secondary literature, and the kinds of materials readily available online are likely to hinder contact between teacher and student. They deliver a ready-made view of the world that tends to remain anonymous, since it is the result of assumptions and value judgments not undertaken by the teacher him- or herself. For this reason Waldorf schools—mainly in the high school—use these materials only to a very limited extent, and then primarily for the purpose of review or encouraging individual work.

"Active" materials: Readers, primary literature, anthologies, original documents and articles, statistics, and reference books are all used in upper elementary and high-school lessons. Besides learning to use such materials, students should learn how to take notes, summarize them for their own use, describe and document processes and procedures, and be able to compare and contrast.

Learning to document one's own learning in this way provides a basis for individual engagement with the subject at hand. It takes different forms:

- In the early grades/primary school, guided by the class teacher, the children begin by writing and drawing the essentials of the lesson content in a blank *main lesson book.* To an appropriate extent, its format is left to their own discretion. Gradually, they take more and more responsibility for both the text and the graphics, which will be subject to aesthetic considerations; thus the book starts to become an expression of individual involvement with the academic material. In high school, the design and content of the main lesson book rests entirely in the hands of the students, and may be transformed into quite other formats.

A main lesson book is intended to be an expression of active, individual learning.

- As a learning medium, the main lesson book can also be supplemented, replaced, or intensified by *portfolio work* (cf. Iwan 2005). Whatever a student finds in connection with a particular subject in the way of texts, pictures, notes taken during conversations, sketches of ideas, etc., are all collected in a portfolio; they are then sifted through, ordered, evaluated, and sometimes even presented. "With the help of a portfolio students discover their own individual learning path and find out what it means to work independently and take responsibility for their own learning." (Brunner 2002, p. 57) It goes without saying that a project like this entails a lot more than simply replacing the main lesson book with a large folder.

CHAPTER 5

REMEDIAL TEACHING (EDUCATIONAL SUPPORT)

"Culture will become more and more unhealthy and humanity will be faced with an increasing need to use the educational process as a way of healing its harmful effects."[14]

— *Rudolf Steiner*

Remedial teaching primarily involves discovering the causes of particular learning and developmental difficulties, and finding appropriate ways to guide the learning process of individual children.

In Waldorf schools, one may regularly encounter children who display behavioral patterns that identify them as needing some sort of learning support. These patterns may appear on a social, physical, emotional, or cognitive level. The purpose of remediation—like any aspect of the Waldorf program—is to further the development of the child's personality, to awaken confidence in his or her own abilities and to improve his or her social skills. This entails close cooperation between teachers, parents, the school doctor, and therapists.

---
14 Steiner (1976), GA 294, Lecture 10

The process begins with discussions in which the child's state of development is considered from a variety of perspectives. Medical check-ups are also very helpful at this stage. They may take place at the time of school admission, and many schools also require them in second and fourth grades in order to monitor children's development. In this way, case histories can be built up so that remedial measures can be undertaken where appropriate.

Remedial teaching is mainly concerned with:

- developing motor coordination
- awakening the senses
- integrating retained primitive reflexes
- encouraging motivation for learning
- schooling auditory and visual perception
- overcoming difficulties with writing and arithmetic

Work on motoric coordination involves the recapitulation of early movement patterns, repeating them in a way compatible with the current age of the child.

Bringing the "lower senses" into their proper state of maturity promotes in the child a sense of inner being, as well as providing the sheer enjoyment of feeling the power of movement and attaining a relaxed upright posture. It also harmonizes the life processes of the body and helps the child feel safe and at home in the world.

Allowing early childhood reflexes to run their course, while at the same time integrating them, prevents them from interfering with motoric, behavioral, and learning development.

Through the improvement of auditory and visual perception, the child develops a feeling of inner well-being in relation to experience and understanding of his or her surroundings.

In the case of difficulties with arithmetic, the remedial teacher works to awaken the child's innate sense of number, rhythm, pattern, and mathematical capacity, for example by helping with counting, regrouping, estimating, and set recognition.

In the case of language arts difficulties, basic sensory-motor and speech exercises are combined with lessons in phonemic awareness, syllabication to help the child progress in speaking, reading, writing, and spelling.

It is not always necessary to approach problems with writing and arithmetic directly, since the difficulties often lie at other levels.

A remedial lesson should always be structured in such a way that it addresses the whole person.

CHAPTER 6

CULTURAL INTEGRATION, INCLUSIVENESS
WORK IN PROGRESS

Pedagogical principles, educational aims, and curriculum

In its basic intentions, Waldorf education is fundamentally inclusive of all children. Diversity is central to the life of a Waldorf school, and finds its expression in some of its main pedagogical features, such as orientation toward the practical, the individualization of learning, and the diversification of learning forms.

A thorough grounding in the study of human development and its methodological and practical classroom implications takes precedence over any kind of fixed curricular guidelines. Here human development is understood from two different sides: On the one hand, the *general* aspects of child development must be taken into account; on the other, attention must always be paid to the characteristics of each *individual* child.

This aspiration to a "both-and" way of working prompts the following questions: What lesson content and methods can relate to all students? And, by the same token, which content, methods, and school structures are likely to exclude certain students in particular circumstances?

The UN Convention on the Rights of the Disabled, which has been in force in the European Union since 2009, stipulates—according to its very specific rules of compliance—new standards that apply to education. The basic aim of inclusiveness requires the integration of children and young people of different nationalities, world-views, social backgrounds, and health conditions, going far beyond the integration of learners with disabilities.

The Waldorf curriculum supports the individual developmental needs of each child. In the first edition of this guide to the Waldorf curriculum, it was stated at the outset that learning and development of the child cannot be externally controlled; rather, it is a question of nurturing the child's inner individually unfolding, imitative impulses toward learning. (Richter 2003, p.34) Pedagogical freedom was named as the highest principle of Waldorf education: every teacher, on the basis of Steiner's lecture cycle on *The Foundations of Human Experience,* has autonomy in the matters of lesson design and methodology. From this arises the conception of the teacher as practitioner of the art of education.

An inclusive Waldorf school could come about through the merging and further development of the qualities of general Waldorf education and those of curative or remedial education. It would be based upon curricula spanning different forms of schooling, alternative methods of assessment, and individualized forms of learning.

Due to the legal requirements for inclusive education, Waldorf schools will have to take a new look at themselves if they are to be truly comprehensive: Can Waldorf education find within itself the resolve to make itself truly available for everyone? The freedom of the individual teacher, the cooperative study of contemporary issues, and precise observations of children are some of the special ingredients that could combine to help teachers create lessons that are holistic and oriented toward today's children. To act in the spirit of freedom and to design lessons out of their own powers of intuition, teachers need, on the one hand, to precisely observe children's individual development and, on the other, to deepen their understanding through child studies with colleagues.

To this end it will be necessary in the coming years to undertake practical research to demonstrate the practicability and consequent effectiveness of inclusive Waldorf education.

CHAPTER 7

COOPERATION WITH CURATIVE SCHOOLS
WORK IN PROGRESS

Waldorf education is open to all children and adolescents. In the first Waldorf school, there were children in need of special care. To meet the needs of these children in a more appropriate way, Rudolf Steiner set up a so-called "support class" in 1920 and entrusted Karl Schubert with the task of running it.

The children enrolled in this class were the only ones whose schooling was not interrupted by the prohibition of all Waldorf schools during the time of the Nazi regime. Schubert managed to ensure this continuity by teaching in private rooms. After the war, the college of the newly reopened school was not inclined to re-admit Schubert and his support class.

Inspired by the *Curative Education Course* given by Steiner in Dornach, Switzerland in 1924, anthroposophical curative education began to develop in both social service and clinical contexts. In a form adapted to their individual purposes, the Waldorf curriculum and methodology were adopted by schools set up along anthroposophical curative lines. This was because the curriculum follows as its basis the overall course of human development, and takes an artistic approach to all subject areas. Thus, it was felt that this would be appropriate to the educational needs of disabled children of all ages.

After World War II, curative Waldorf schools for children with special needs were founded in addition to mainstream Waldorf schools. They varied in terms of their breadth of curative concern. Some established Waldorf schools included small-sized classes (so-called *Kleinklassen*) for those who needed a special learning environment. There are now schools that are increasingly practicing integration and striving to become fully inclusive. Some current models can be found at www.lehrplan-waldorf.de.

Historically the Waldorf schools in Germany have been affiliated with the *Bund der freien Waldorfschulen* while the curative Waldorf schools belong to the *Anthropoi Bundesverband anthroposophisches Sozialwesen e. V.* The curative schools are free to be active members of both of these organizations.

With the well-being of children always in mind, these associations work together on aspects of Waldorf pedagogy and lend each other mutual support. In 2010, to further this cooperation, a coordinating group was formed of representatives from the associations and a coordination council consisting of regional delegates. This has led, for instance, to the convening of large conferences, sometimes in cooperation with the Medical and Pedagogical Sections at the Goetheanum in Dornach, Switzerland, as well as with professional working groups.

In times when the challenges that special-needs children face are becoming increasingly individual, these types of intensive exchange, mutual support, and cooperation among colleagues in various Waldorf institutions and associations are particularly important for the continuation of appropriate help and care for children and their development.

CHAPTER 8

TEACHING MIXED AGE & CROSS-DISCIPLINARY GROUPS
(ongoing research)

Mixed-age teaching usually means that two adjoining age groups are taught together as a combined class. A growing number of schools have adopted a system of these conjoint classes, with the intention of reaping the pedagogical benefits that accrue from broadening the scope of social relationships. A wealth of experience in this area shows that this form of a school can create a developmentally sound learning environment fully compatible with the foundations of Waldorf education.

Teaching in this way, however, requires identifying the central qualities of Waldorf education and reworking them for use in this new context. Although this task is not new, the issues to be resolved here are different and go to the central question: What is the actual core of Waldorf education? Whatever form this kind of school takes, it must strive as much for an integrated whole as any Waldorf school working with single age-group classes.

As for teaching cross-disciplinary groups, the more the senses of today's children and teenagers are assailed by a flood of digital information and fragmented factual knowledge, the more significant becomes Waldorf education's goal of providing a form of pedagogy that offers a holistic perspective on the relationship between humanity and the world. Among the methods that bridge fragmentation and lead toward a universally human form of understanding, cross-disciplinary teaching plays a key role.

This approach does not proceed from fixed, ready-made definitions, but encourages the children to become actively involved in considering a range of perspectives and viewing them in relation to one another. A teaching method that characterises phenomena in a variety of different—perhaps even opposite—ways demands of both teachers and students a high level of engagement. It takes full cognizance of the young person's need and ability to make and formulate new discoveries in the process of learning. Changes in perspective can lead to wonder, interest, and the joy of discovery; then, out of these, arise lively questions and exploratory thinking, which finally lead to comprehensive understanding.

The potential for crossing disciplinary boundaries is particularly evident in the interaction between history and geography, as it appears, for instance, in the Grade 7 main lesson on the Age of Discovery. In being taken through vivid descriptions of the voyages of Magellan or other adventurers, students experience a variety of subject areas as a multi-contextual unity:

- historical processes
- geographical and climatic conditions and relationships
- geology, biology, zoology, and astronomy
- technical and cartographic inventions and insights
- trade, economics, and transport technology
- ethnology and cultural history

Whatever the subject, the more the teacher succeeds in incorporating apparently unrelated (but ultimately relevant) topics, the more the students are challenged to discover new meanings and to relate to them in terms of their own level of development.

Here are a few examples of how such combinations appear in practice:

- Using the numerical relationships in music for arithmetical purposes in the lower and middle elementary school

- Grade 5 main lesson on ancient cultural epochs in connection with eurythmy

- Acoustics in Grade 6 in connection with music and the construction of instruments

- Nutrition main lesson in Grade 7 together with gardening, geography, biology, economics, mathematics, and medicine

- Foreign or world languages in the upper elementary grades taught in connection with geography and music

- Parzival main lesson in Grade 11 incorporating eurythmy, drama, art, and projective geometry

- Projective geometry in Grade 11 combined with with embryology, ethics, philosophy, literature, and eurythmy

By moving creatively among subjects like this, a young person can come to a concrete experience and knowledge of his or her own selfhood. This establishes a feeling of coherence and confidence in his or her own future ability to enter into a sound relationship between self and world. Such participatory awareness ultimately affects a person's general health and well-being and his or her readiness to take on responsibility in the world.

CHAPTER 9

PERFORMANCE AND EVALUATION

In Waldorf schools the concepts of "performance" and "competition" are seen in pedagogical terms. Two forms of performance are considered desirable: (a) one in which development of individual abilities, talents, and powers of understanding, judgment, and motivation are discernible within the learning process; and (b) one that has more to do with how much each individual has lived up to his or her own potential in terms of attainment and contribution to the social community.

   a In terms of this first definition, singing, music-making, drama, crafts, and art are not evaluated according to their intrinsic artistic worth, but as the outcome of an activity (which could equally well be cognitive in nature) that is part of a student's overall educational growth. In arriving at the level of performance, the young person will have been in competition not with others, but with him- or herself. In all subject areas, the evaluation of performance is based on these criteria. Performance evaluation, as a purely quantitative assessment and as a criterion of selection, rather than as the cultivation of talent, is rightly regarded as inhumane. Ideally, educational performance is considered to be no different from, say, professional performance, for which abilities and talents are also under constant development. This kind of performance evaluation naturally entails a descriptive verbal report, not a normative set of marks.

b In keeping with the second definition, the attempt is made to ensure that students, especially in the high school, learn to appreciate performance as an end in itself, and motivate themselves accordingly.

In many countries, Waldorf schools are expected to prepare students for state-recognized examinations. Since Waldorf schools do not classify students according to performance, each class will contain students preparing for a wide variety of examinations. Since the Waldorf curriculum does not match state school curricula, this sometimes means that special preparation courses for certain subjects have to be introduced. For both teachers and students, this kind of teaching is always a compromise.

Reports

At the end of every school year, teachers write a report for every child they have taught. This report is intended to give the parents or guardians a picture of their child's development and a realistic idea of his or her progress. As the children grow older, the report may also be addressed to them. In composing a report, the teacher reviews his or her overall experience of each child in a nonjudgmental way. The composition of these descriptions may pose a considerable challenge for the teacher, in terms of finding formulations that provide clear and factual—and yet suitably appreciative—pictures, so that the parents or guardians gain an accurate impression of how things stand with their child's education. "This is why the report that we give out for each child at the end of the school year looks like a little biography [...] of all the experiences we have had of the child throughout the year both in and out of the classroom." (Steiner 1979: GA 305, p.152) There is, of course, no question here of an individual child being compared to others, or measured against some general standard, although particular behavioral quirks will always appear and be remarked upon within the context of the class community as a whole. Some elementary school teachers begin to give letter or number grades as their students enter the upper elementary years.

In the report, the teacher attempts to describe the learner's progress in such a way that perspectives for future development also come to expression. Writing a report effectively means being concerned with the question: "What predispositions does a particular person have, and what can be developed?" (Steiner 1982: GA 24, p. 37) If, in the teacher's characterization, the parents recognize their own experience of their child, this can form the basis of a relationship of trust through which their joint educational responsibility can be constantly renewed.

PART II

THE WALDORF CURRICULUM VIEWED "HORIZONTALLY"
Grades 1–12

CHAPTER 1

HORIZONTAL AND VERTICAL CURRICULUM:
A Comparison

The horizontal curriculum is an attempt to describe all the chief lesson content appropriate for each phase of child and adolescent development year by year. Here, of course, the children and adolescents should be regarded not merely as recipients, but much more as the motivators of the lesson content—as the original commissioners, so to speak, of the curriculum.

By virtue of its generalized character, the horizontal curriculum tends to be rather light on specific detail and unavoidably fragmentary. It is in the vertical curriculum that descriptions of lesson content become more detailed and distinct, and the methodological implications of each subject's details become much more clearly discernible. The relative time spent on various aspects of a particular subject in both the horizontal and the vertical curricula can be established only on the basis of a pedagogically applied understanding of the human being as a whole.

Before addressing the broad outlines of the curriculum horizontally and each of the subjects of the curriculum seen vertically from Grades 1–12, we must delineate the main features of child development upon which the curriculum is based. Rudolf Steiner addresses these developmental features in his *Foundations of Human Experience*. His conclusions regarding "categories which structure observation and disclose phenomenological novelties" serve to facilitate "new insights into the articulations of human growth, as well as increased awareness of one's own capacities for the attainment of knowledge ..." (Rittelmeyer 2010, p. 9f.)

If the horizontal curriculum calls forth the desire for detail and systematic order, the vertical could perhaps be said to elicit the need to see the whole picture.

As all good architecture takes account of the needs of the people who have to live or work in it, and perhaps also seeks to express its function through the originality of its form, so the architecture or composition of the Waldorf school curriculum is realized only—in a completely individual way and under constantly changing conditions—through the living and dynamic interplay between its horizontal and vertical structural principles.

CHAPTER 2

BACKGROUND TO TEACHING IN THE ELEMENTARY-SCHOOL GRADES

Before embarking on our survey of the theoretical background to teaching in the elementary and ultimately high-school grades, we should briefly take a look at the early childhood or preschool years.

The time before children are "ready for school"[15]—normally up to the age of six or seven—is characterized by particularly intense sensory activity, which has direct internal effects: the child is completely bound up with whatever happens in his or her immediate surroundings. Many essential learning and developmental processes are founded upon this early facility for (unconscious) imitation. Learning to walk, speak, and think are all occasioned by such participatory experience of the surrounding world. The maturing organs of the child's inherited "body template" attain their distinctive individualized structures in the same way, directly influenced by what happens in the child's surroundings and by the effects of his or her own activity (cf. Kranich

---

15 These words have been placed in quotation marks because the concept of "school readiness" is viewed from a variety of theoretical perspectives—in developmental terms, in terms of the theory of learning, or in systemic interactionist terms (see Pehm 2015, p. 15ff.)—and the present context does not permit the drawing of such fine distinctions. Currently, all these conceptual options are widely used in the realm of Waldorf education. Nonetheless, when a child is described as "ready for school," both parents and teachers have a clear idea of what they are talking about—namely, that the child "meets the individual requirements for starting school." (Wagner et al. 2010, p. 8)

1999). These processes of organic transformation bear witness to the effective presence of a self-activating individual. Recognising this presence within the process of development is of crucial importance for all aspects of learning.

In a previous chapter, the threefold conception of the human organism, which forms the basis of anthroposophical anthropology, was sketched in outline. It showed how the self, the "I," the central entity of human individuality, has to come to terms with the physical body (and its life processes) as well as the emotional and mental aspects of this organism. Accordingly, at preschool age the main objective is to ensure that the child is able to fully develop his or her physical body and life processes. To this end, the child's development needs to be in the hands of dependable, open-hearted nurturers, who in their care and concern for the child's well-being can engender a feeling of security and set a good example.

By around the age of seven, the re-shaping of the child's organs is largely complete. An external sign of this is the shedding of the milk teeth. "The sculptural processes by which the second teeth are formed are linked to other formative processes, which can be summed up under the heading of the first growth spurt. Bound up with both the change of teeth and the growth spurt are well-known, far-reaching developmental steps on the path toward psychological and physical maturity. The formative forces which had been active in the organism up to this point have now finished their transformative work; that which they previously shaped, they now only have to maintain. The maintenance of a building is much less taxing than its construction. Thus these formative forces can now become involved in other tasks." (Leber 1993, p. 248)

Steiner discovered that these same early sculptors of the bodily organs later become the foundation of all learning. He describes how, after "the building has been given shape," these sculptural forces do not disappear but seek out new fields of activity as the forces of thinking. "It is of paramount significance to know that the human being's ordinary powers of thought are the refined forces of growth and form ..." (Steiner/Wegmann 1991, GA 27, p. 12) This, then, is the meaning of being "ready for school": it now becomes possible to have free rather than situational memory, to form mental pictures, and build up an inner world of personal feeling and experience. If children are confronted by formal learning before this time, as is happening more and more nowadays with the gradual lowering of the school starting-age, this can lead to a general weakening of the child's constitution later in life.

In the organism as a whole, the years that follow are concerned largely with growth processes.

THE CHILD BETWEEN THE AGES OF SEVEN AND NINE

At the interview for admission into Grade one, which takes place when children are six or seven years old, teachers check for sufficient limb growth (first growth spurt) and bodily coordination, as well as the ability to remember and retell spoken narrative and copy simple forms. It is also important to assess whether the child is emotionally ready to step out of the familiar security of family and kindergarten. It must be said, of course, that obtaining a clear picture of whether a child is "ready for school" is becoming increasingly difficult and demands a practiced eye. Many aspects of modern civilization strongly affect children's behavior and ability to express themselves. As a result, a dissociation of the various developmental levels may become apparent: intellectual acuity may signal readiness for school, while physical, emotional, and social development lag behind. Research into human resilience shows that a child's health and inclination toward life-long learning is promoted neither by intellectual instruction nor by cognitive reflection, but rather by cultivating (bringing to maturity) the emotional and volitional life.

Many child psychologists and educational theorists speak of a "destandardization of childhood" in connection with a variety of childhood behavior patterns (Honig 2002, p. 325 and Ullrich 2010, p. 116). In their criticism of Waldorf education's view of childhood, they seem to overlook the fact that Waldorf teachers take this diverse picture very much for granted. Waldorf education, however, does not take its lead solely from the manifold phenomena of new patterns of child behavior, but seeks to derive its method and content from the deeper levels of child development, just as Steiner suggested in 1907 in his ground-breaking essay *The Education of the Child in the Light of Anthroposophy* (Steiner 1987). In practice, this means taking full cognizance of the qualities of the modern child, and from there proceeding to explore the "subtext" of the child.

Between the ages of seven and nine, this subtext expresses itself as a pronounced eagerness to learn. Memory, imagination, enjoyment of rhythmic repetition, and often a hunger for imaginative stories about the world at large (the full range of natural, social, and cultural fields of learning and experience) are all available to be activated. At this age children still naturally look up to adults, but no longer simply through direct, imitative, sensory experience, but rather through their relationship to a particular person who is seen as being exemplary in word and deed. The questions the child carries within and directs toward the teacher are also part of the "subtext." They could well be formulated as: "Do you really see me?" and "Can you help me get to know the world?" In effect, these questions challenge the teacher to create and develop an inner relationship to the child. Answering these basic questions takes place through the lessons, the aim of which is not only to present a narrative *about* the world, but to deliver a direct encounter *with* the world, so that from the experience of wonder thus evoked the children come to reflect upon it. If children feel that what they are offered meets these basic needs, then the teacher will have "passed the test" and will be accepted as a figure of loving authority.

In the time between the change of teeth and puberty, teachers can contribute a great deal toward children's development by approaching them in an artistic way, e.g. through pictures—not only externally visible ones, but mainly verbal imagery, in other words stories that evoke inner pictures. But it doesn't stop there: "artistic" in the full scope of its meaning implies a union of idea and will that combine to shape material through an active inner as well as outer process, such that within the sensory the non-sensory appears. For this to happen within a teaching context, music, sculpture, artistic movement, painting, poetry, and drama must all work together. "Artistic," however, also means paying due attention to the timing and dramatic construction of a lesson: if something is to be grasped by *thinking*, it should also—probably beforehand—be combined with *feeling*, in order then to be put into practical *action*. The balanced and vibrant interplay of these three elements is not experienced as tiring, but as animating and healthy.

It is worth pointing out that the earlier imitative phase lingers into the first two or three years of elementary school. All learning will be affected by this, and lessons should create an experiential context allowing for it; progress in cognitive learning should not be placed at a higher premium than advances in the social, affective, and volitional realms. The consciousness of the child at this phase of life, which can be closely associated with what Jean Gebser described as the magical-mythical mind-structure (cf. Gebser 1986), does not yet make a clear distinction between self and world. The latter is experienced not as environment, but in a participatory mode in which there are no sharp boundaries between the living and the dead, the animate and the inanimate.

THE CHILD BETWEEN THE AGES OF NINE AND TWELVE

At around the age of nine, i.e., in the third or fourth year of elementary school, the child experiences a disruption in the feeling of unity with the world.[16] He or she becomes aware of a separation between self and world, between self and the adult world. This may result in a first experience of acute loneliness. The teacher's authority, which has so far been treated as if it were a law of nature, is now called into question. The child wants to know whether the teacher's articulate assurance, which was formerly accepted as a matter of course, really rests upon a comprehensive knowledge of the world. This question, of course, is not always put into words; sometimes it remains below the level of verbal expression. Nonetheless, it is perfectly discernible in the children's behavior. For the teacher, this presents a considerable educational challenge: those aspects of the world which are brought into school (the lesson content) must take into account the above-mentioned separation, while the teaching method must help the child on the journey from a magical "golden land" of early childhood into the "full Technicolor" of the physical world. An authentic encounter with the world is not to be equated with depersonalized scientific abstractions. The stronger the feeling of the "loss of paradise" becomes, the more emphatically must the human being be presented as the central point of reference: "But you will have to relate everything to the human being [....] Everything you present the child with, when you tell him a fable and apply it to the human being, when in natural history you relate the squid and the mouse to the human being, when in connection with the Morse telegraph you evoke a feeling of what a wonder has been achieved with the laying of the cables in the earth—all these are things which connect the whole world in its particulars with the human being." (Steiner 1992, GA 293, p. 141)

Once the child has crossed this "Rubicon," a new phase of development begins. This lasts roughly until the age of twelve. Before the second growth spurt takes fully hold, through extensive growth of the lungs, a deeper, more relaxed breathing rhythm is established. This physiological change seems to be correlated with a change in

---

16 Steiner often designates this developmental step as the Rubicon, alluding to the historical event when Julius Caesar crossed the Rubicon River in Northern Italy, and in so doing irrevocably broke traditional Roman law and emancipated himself from it in the process (cf. Steiner 1990, GA 294, p. 106).

emotional disposition. There appears to be a special harmony and equanimity in the child's feeling life, which no longer expresses itself in wilful outbursts. Rather the dynamic seems to work in the opposite direction: openness to the world complemented by caring attention. It is no mistake to choose for this special time of transition, designated by many as the "high point of childhood" (Schiller 2005, p. 100), the term *balance*. This, of course, also implies that this state is precarious.

The body soon loses the structural harmony that characterizes the middle of childhood, for with the release of sex hormones a growth spurt stronger than the previous one sets in. Skeletal growth increases, especially in the limbs, and muscle formation intensifies. The task is now to take control of this radically changing body.

The self-assertion that accompanies this growth spurt expresses itself as a critical attitude, especially toward the adult world; but it is also associated with renewed and perhaps even more intense feelings of loneliness and vulnerability. In this process of forging a personal identity, a major component is, of course, the massive influence of peer groups and the media, which inculcate standard images of youth culture that are very difficult for the rising generation to resist (cf. Götte et al. 2009, p. 141ff.).

What the child on the threshold of adolescence experiences as highly charged emotions and aspirations stands in strong contrast to the now clearly discernible faculty of causal thinking. The awakening intellect is stepping into its rightful place, and the challenge now is to provide it with sufficient opportunities for active engagement with the world.

PREADOLESCENCE: AGE TWELVE TO FOURTEEN

In this time of searching and intense experience of his or her own soul life, the student's natural curiosity is directed toward the physical world. Of course, the human being—not an impersonal instrument of measurement—is still the primary medium of research, investigation, and discovery; but still, the student now wants to discover laws that exist and retain their validity independently of the human being. However, it is not only this demand for knowledge of the structure of the physical world that must be met. There is also a need to know about the structure of time, as, for instance, in historical processes. The human being both shapes and is shaped by history, and historical data are not organized in terms of quantitative abstractions.

As regards "shaping" in a personal sense, it is precisely at times when nothing is happening outwardly that there is intense inner activity (brooding, rumination). The power of decision-making and the ability to order one's own life have to be discovered individually. To overcome their limitations, young people must be able to activate their own will. This represents, not least, a considerable challenge to the power of imagination, which needs to be called upon again and again at this age, precisely because it offers the possibility of using the bottom line (facts) not as a sofa, but more as a trampoline.

The culmination of this developmental phase is the transition to adolescence. This used to be identified with puberty, but there is strong evidence that in the industrialized world over the last century and a half biological maturity is happening earlier, whereas psychological maturity has not kept pace with this acceleration and may even be correspondingly delayed (cf. Knussmann 1996).

Helpful experiences during this period of development are assignments that present young people with physical and social challenges that lead them to discover their own strength, while at the same time, by virtue of their having performed a necessary service, show them that they are needed in the world. Erhard Fucke, a strong advocate for an educational model that integrates general education with vocational training, puts it this way: "The primary task in preadolescence is the education of the will. It is only by meeting this demand that preadolescents can gradually stand on their own two feet and come to feel at home in the 'world outside.' Only insofar as they are fully engaged in a specific activity in the world can they arrive at ever new inner experience of their partial, sovereign independence in relation to the world. They also gain the experience that in principle this sovereignty can be extended, albeit that every extension will mean hard work." (Fucke 1993, p. 48)

Preadolescents wish to find their way in the world and often feel isolated, and so they need to be given orientation through a holistic worldview. Much more than before they develop an interest in interrelationships between traditional branches of knowledge.

If in Grades 1–3 the teacher concentrates on making "the universal" intelligible for the children in his or her words, and if the second phase of education is more dedicated to bringing the phenomena of the world into dialogue with the human being, then what is required for the time of outward inarticulateness (preadolescence) is the ability to listen to the inner language, the hidden words of these young people and, on this basis, to open up new "avenues of articulation" for them.

CHAPTER 3

HORIZONTAL CURRICULUM OF THE ELEMENTARY-SCHOOL YEARS

TRANSITIONAL CLASSES

The step from kindergarten to elemenetary school represents an important biographical turning point. To know whether a child is ready for it, kindergarten teachers need to keep a watchful eye on a range of developmental indicators. At kindergarten age, the character and method of education are closely bound up with the bodily growth processes of the young child. The child answers the promptings of his or her surroundings with imitation, imaginative play, and, above all, with the formation of local or situational memory, all of which serve to nurture the forces of health and individual will. Placing premature educational demands on the child's cognitive abilities disturbs and weakens these growth processes.

With the change of teeth, a transformation of existential proportions sets in: the formative forces, which up to now have been working within the organic processes of the body undergo a reorientation and can now be taken advantage of for the purposes of learning and memory. Since this transformational relationship between processes of bodily and mental development is very individual in character, the conversations between primary and kindergarten teachers and parents on the matter of school readiness require enough space and time for detailed observations of the children to be made. If it is felt that children of six going on seven have outgrown the kindergarten, but in their development are still not quite ready for the full "dynamics" of school—i.e. constant alternation between group activity, attentive listening, and independent work—then a school has the option to introduce a so-called transitional or pre-school class. Here the children's particular level of development will be closely observed, and classes will provide:

- varied stimulation and training of the senses

- training of motor coordination in guided activities and play

- development of social and language skills through a variety of activities

- promotion of health through the rhythmic structuring of the day, with attention paid to both individual and community development

GRADES 1 TO 3

Many children arrive at school with great expectations. They have high hopes for answers to big "How" and "Why" questions to help them on their way in the world. If these answers are sufficiently imaginative to satisfy the children's imaginations—helping them form and transform inner pictures based on experience—then they can begin to feel at home and accepted in this world. This is only possible when the child engages his or her will and actively connects with every aspect of schoolwork.

"It comes to no less than this, that between the child's seventh and fourteenth years, we have to bring his thinking into a right relationship with his will, with his willing. [...] The whole character of the human being, in so far as it proceeds from the inner being, depends upon a true harmony being established by human activity between thinking and willing." (Steiner 1986, GA 307, p. 88)

Form drawing, a subject unknown in most any mainstream school curriculum,[17] illustrates what is involved here: straight and curved forms are described as far as possible using the whole body (in walking, large arm and hand movements), and then carried out as drawings, coming to rest, as it were, on paper. This demands of children concentrated control in a realm where they are in their element: that of movement. These forms are not pictures of anything; in this respect they are "meaningless." The whole focus is on the quality of a particular form, which is understood by feel and touch, using the finger. Experiencing many things for the first time, in both emotional and volitional terms, is one of the fundamental features of the first three years of school; in addition, form drawing is of inestimable value for the purpose of learning to write, because it teaches the child about graphic orientation on a page. In the second and third years of school, these basic drawing exercises are supplemented by others involving symmetry, patterns, and guided freehand work. Within the qualitative experience of drawing, cognitive and will activities are taken in the direction of feeling; in other words, feeling is appealed to as an organ of perception. (cf. Bühler 2000)

The qualitative aspect of form is also a feature of the initial stages of lessons in *language arts,* or lessons concerning the child's mother tongue (sometimes called "home language" lessons). Here the focus is on experiencing the qualities of sounds, rhymes, and rhythms, as well as the shapes and meanings of letters. In deriving the form of a letter from a pictorial illustration (consonant) or an inwardly evoked mood image (vowel), the child develops an individual relationship to

---

17 The order in which subjects are presented in this outline is neither schematic nor arbitrary. The attempt has been made to place at the beginning the subject with characteristic features that best represent the grade level concerned. For the rest of the sequence, the subjects are intended either to follow naturally from their predecessors or, through contrast, to bring out essential developmental or thematic perspectives.

each individual letter, and, subsequently, to the whole activity of writing. In these first lessons, it is especially important that the children's interest is awakened by a method that starts from the whole, enabling them to make connections, say, between a phonemic sound and a particular animal or plant.

In Grade 2, following the introduction of capital letters in first grade, lower-case letters are introduced so that, at the latest by Grade 3, the transition can be made to longhand or cursive writing. (In some English-speaking schools it has become common, by means of dynamic form drawing, to go straight to the learning of longhand writing in Grade 2.) It is also increasingly recommended that lower-case letters are introduced in Grade 1. The second year is also the time when readers are first used. Before this time, children read only what they have written themselves. Right from year one every opportunity is taken to encourage the children to write things themselves, according to their own capabilities. Grammar teaching begins in Grade 3 with a view to enabling the children to distinguish different types of sentences and the basic parts of speech (noun, adjective, verb, etc.).

At this level, the teaching of *foreign languages* (also called **world languages**) is as important as learning about one's native tongue. From first grade on, children usually have lessons in two (living) foreign languages, taught by the oral method of listening, speaking, singing, etc. In these lessons there is as yet no writing or formal grammar. Rather, the idea is that through poems, stories, songs, and games, the children get to "bathe" in the foreign language. In this way they experience another way of perceiving the world. This is one of the most important prerequisites for the ability later on to form flexible concepts and a comprehensive worldview.

The **narrative material** or **story curriculum**[18] serves to create "the child's path onto the earth and into the world." In the *fairy tale* (Grade one) the totality of the human being, animal, nature, and suprasensory

---

[18] The story themes given here are the purview of the class teacher; they provide an orientation for the subject teachers.

world is experienced. In Grade two this differentiates into *fables* (the human being's "lower nature") and *legends* (the human being's "higher nature"). In Grade three, in stories taken from the great traditions of religion, the child experiences human beings in their responsibility toward the earth and toward the divine. In Christian cultures, these stories can be taken from *Genesis* and stories from the *Old Testament;* in other cultural milieus—for instance, Buddhist, Hindu, Jewish, or Moslem—other texts will be chosen.

Elementary science in Grade 3, with its two main themes of farming and house building, represents another signpost along this "path into the world." It should involve the children in the actual practicalities of land cultivation the construction of shelters. In preparation for this the teacher also has the task of awakening the children's awareness of certain phenomena in the world of nature, so that they can take part in observing the passage of the day and year. Obviously, these lessons will draw their content from the school's immediate surroundings. Age-appropriate insights gained in this year of school prepare the child to understand economic and ecological relationships later in life.

In *arithmetic,* the element of movement experienced earlier in form drawing appears again in rhythmic counting, and attention to the special qualities of forms reappears in the introduction of numbers. A qualitative approach also applies to discovering the four basic arithmetical operations. Beginning from the whole (the sum) and not from single quantities (Steiner 1990: GA 294, p. 13f, 72), children engage in practical experiences such as sharing out, comparing sizes, giving and taking things away, etc. Everything the children do in this way is written down. The written forms of arithmetic operations are dealt with in Grade 3. The times tables (at first experienced through movement or developed out of rhythmic skip-counting) and mental arithmetic are intensively practiced right from first grade.

Qualitative first-hand experience: this is also what *water-color painting* is about. The aim is to lead the child toward experience of the inner tones of colors and the feelings they evoke. What inner qualities belong to the three primary colors of blue, yellow, and red? The purpose of painting lessons is not to reproduce external objects or create pictorial illustrations, but to explore the realm of feeling and "listen to the inner language" of colors.

Just as painting has to do with sensing the tones of colors, so *music* in the first three years is about experiencing the colors of individual tones and tonal atmospheres. Here it is important for the child not to focus solely on one inner mood that lives, for instance, in the diatonic scale or in major-minor tonality. Rather, tonal experience should inhabit a more open space, for instance the pentatonic scale or "mood of the fifth." In using instruments such as the pentatonic flute, recorder, kinderharp, or lyre, at first the only pieces played are those that the children have already learned to sing. The first steps in musical notation begin in Grade 3 in conjunction with the transition from pentatonic to diatonic music based upon a fundamental tone (the tonic note of the diatonic scale), or using a scale appropriate to the local culture (in conjunction with the corresponding instruments). While the recorder requires control of the breath, something essentially new arises when string instruments are added to the music curriculum. Whereas before both hands were directly involved in relation to the breath, with string instruments the right hand does the bowing while the left does the fingering and the ear does the correcting, introducing an element of manual finesse, like that of a skilled craftsperson. Music is a time-related art, which means that music lessons provide an experience of structured time.

Eurythmy combines both spatial and temporal dimensions in that the sounds of language and music are made visible through bodily movements and forms moved in space. The child lives within the tension of sensory alertness and the tendency to simply go with the actions of the body. By appealing to the child's feelings, this art is particularly well suited to harmonizing this tension. Eurythmy helps children, both individually and in groups, become sure-footed in relation to the three dimensions of space; in this way—as with music and games—it is of great social significance.

In the first three years of school *gymnastics* lead children to an experience of their own body and its capacity to move. The first two years are devoted to nurturing the child's bodily agility in a playful way. This chiefly involves learning and practicing circle and movement games, most of which have a strong social component. In Grade 3, the transition is made to "proper" gymnastics in that previously practiced movement exercises are now directed more toward a specific purpose.

In *handwork* the emphasis is likewise on developing bodily dexterity in both boys and girls. The general educational aim of training fine motor coordination is not gender-specific. The practice of such coordination also corresponds with neuronal development of the brain (cf. Steiner 1971, GA 302, p. 69; Wilson 2000). In these artistic-practical lessons the children make items of practical use such as potholders, hats, bags, etc.

The main characteristics of these three years of school can be summarized in this way: They are concerned with setting children on the path into the world, while also giving due consideration to their basic need to experience the "inner side" of nature, of language, of music, and of various human cultural skills. It is important that children learn to feel admiration and respect not only for the wonders of the world as it is, but also for those who possess creative know-how. In this way, in addition to feeling at home in the world, children develop the desire to have accomplished something, and this feeling gives the child's learning a reason and goal.

If the preschool age child needs physical movement, with the change of teeth an internal counterpart is now added to external movement. In everything that is experienced and memorized pictorially, an active inner process is involved. Eager participation in the content of lessons should alternate with quiet reflection upon what has been accomplished. In creating such an interplay, the teacher is fulfilling his or her task of teaching the child "how to breathe properly" (Steiner 1992: GA 293, p. 25).

GRADES 4 TO 6

At the latest, by Grade 4 we find that the child's soul life has undergone a radical change. The relationship to nature and to people in general has become more distant. No longer at one with the world, the child has come to experience the world as a surrounding environment: "And the point at which the child turns nine is particularly important because here, as at a significant biographical turning point, questions begin shooting out of the child, whole heaps of questions, as it were. They all have to do with the child's inner need to distinguish him- or herself from the surrounding world and from the teacher. [...] These questions do not need to be voiced, but they are there. Inwardly the child is asking whether the teacher is properly equipped for life, whether the teacher has a secure hold on life, whether he knows what he wants, and above all the child has a subtle sense for the quality of the teacher's character." (Steiner 1987: GA 303, p. 178)

Whereas the child previously experienced time and space as a unity, now he or she can begin to grasp how they can be structured. For instance, the historical origins of spatial phenomena can be explored (as in local geography), relating "before" and "after" to each other. Usually by the age of twelve (Grade 6) the moment has arrived when the child seeks not only to know the causes of things, but also to be a causal agent and to observe the effects of his or her actions.

The implications of these developments for curricular content will be presented in what follows.

In language lessons, the process of looking at grammatical structuring of time begins, and this applies as much to the teaching of the child's native tongue as of *foreign language:* "Now, before the age of nine the child's relationship to language is based entirely on feeling. But his or her self-confidence could not develop if we did not bring in something of a cognitive element. This is why it is so necessary to introduce the child to the cognitive element. It is done by the roundabout route of grammatical rules, taught in some suitably sensible way. Primarily this applies to the child's mother tongue, but, of course, it could equally well be done in relation to a foreign language." (Steiner 1987: GA 303, p. 206) This implies that writing in the foreign language has already begun; in Russian, this entails the introduction of the Cyrillic script.

In working with verb tenses, language's relation to time is experienced and understood. As the child's soul life grows in complexity, lessons in the language arts provide verbal forms capable of giving it expression. The child experiences not only the grammatical equivalents of changes of perspective and relationship, but also—in the distinctions between direct and indirect speech and between active and passive voice—the ways in which one's own position is defined (Grade 5). Further facets of grammar open up in Grade 6 with the exploration of the conditional tense, by which distinctions among wish, intention, and reality can be made. The relationship to reality is also strengthened by the composition of business letters. In foreign language teaching, corresponding examples might be conversational exercises using practical situations from everyday life.

Music also involves a kind of grammar through the experience of temporal and spatial aspects of tonal structures. This includes time values in musical notation (taught in conjunction with fractions in Grade 4) and the relationship between tonic, dominant, and sub-dominant chords. This leads—not in terms of music theory but in a directly practical way—to an appreciation of the concept of cadence. Musical experience is then extended into music-making in several voices, first with the canon and then moving to simple polyphony. The difference between major and minor moods, created by the intervals of major and minor thirds, is worked on from the fifth school year onwards. Alternatively, of course, it is possible in all these instances to use scales and structures germane to the local culture.

Eurythmy interacts in many different ways with other subjects. In tone eurythmy the focus is on the various keys associated with the circle of fifths, together with exercises on intervals and rhythms; in speech eurythmy, attention is paid to grammatical forms. Verses, poems, ballads that may figure in history or local geography lessons will also be converted into speech eurythmy. In walking circles, hexagons, triangles, etc. as well as doing exercises with rods, there is an obvious connection with the geometry lessons of Grades 5 and 6.

Just as the ***arithmetic*** lessons of Grade 1 were derived from the unity of One, in Grade 4 this subject has a similar point of departure. The unity, the totality, breaks into pieces, although the parts (fractions) have a lawful relation to the whole. Fractions display not only quantitative relationships but can also be imagined in relation to time, as has been mentioned in the section on music. Via decimal numbers and decimal fractions (Grade 5) the path leads—as preparation for causal logic—to the calculation of interest and percentages: the first mathematical investigation of causes. From calculations involving business transactions in connection with economics, algebra is gradually introduced.

Freehand ***form drawing*** now gains a strong structural component in the drawing of ornamental knots or lattice-like patterns. The aim is to combine beauty with precision, which requires alert attention and can help a fourth grader develop weaving and interconnecting lines of thought (cf. Schuberth 2008, p. 10, 74). This clearly shows the significance of form drawing in the schooling of thinking, before it blossoms into geometric drawing in Grade 5, albeit initially without ruler and compass. With four years of practice in form drawing, the children have acquired a well-honed sense for the straight line, angle, circle, triangle, etc. The task is now to draw these shapes as accurately as possible as geometric figures. Only when hand and eye have reached a sufficient level of proficiency are compasses introduced, while by way of geometric definitions they become acquainted with the process of formulating proofs. Thinking in terms of causality or cause and effect is also evident as an aspect of black-and-white drawing, which is developed out of *painting*: in Grade 6 water-color painting is joined by *charcoal drawing*, which entails working with the polarity of light and shade. As in freehand geometry, the projection of a shadow has to be accurately sensed before it can be traced and given form with charcoal.

In other subjects this process of differentiation and concretization is equally evident. Elementary science branches out into geography and history, and then gives rise to nature study, comprising main lessons on the human being, animals, plants (with the practical application from Grade 6 on in the form of gardening), and minerals.

Local geography (Grade 4) is concerned with the geographic features of the children's home surroundings, with particular emphasis on their economic implications. Here, attention is paid to the relationship between landscape configuration and soil quality, as well as to their historical changes. *Geography* proper begins in Grade 5 with a consideration of the home country as a whole and its connection to other countries, eventually culminating by the end of elementary school in a short, systematic survey of the whole earth. Social and ecological aspects of this subject, insofar as they touch upon the co-existence of different peoples and human responsibility toward the natural world, play an essential role at this age. Economic issues should also be included. (There is a parallel here to the business letter in language arts classes and conversation exercises in foreign language classes.)

In *astronomy*, which should be seen as closely associated with both local and global geography, the children gain experience in describing observed celestial phenomena. The pictures thus arrived at can be extrapolated in an attempt to grasp the configuration of the heavens in relation to the entire earth. Thus "the children come to understand that the face and vegetation of the earth are determined by what they have learned in class […] of 'what goes on in the sky'" (Fucke 1993, p. 175).

History begins as a distinct subject once the pupils are capable of detaching from the present moment and forming ideas of time. Initially, the entry into history is located far back in the mythical realm of Ancient India, and then taken further with presentations of the ancient cultures of Mesopotamia, Egypt, and Greece. In Grade 6, the children are first introduced to the history of the Romans, and thence to the Middle Ages. Thus they hear how the culture of Europe was changed by such events as the Crusades (here again the principle of causality looms large!). "The Occident lagged behind the Orient in many respects. All that developed so well in the way of industrial activity in the towns of Italy and even in towns further to the north was thanks to the Crusades. Here you can conjure up pictures of the spiritual progress of culture at this time." (Steiner 1984: GA 295, p. 79)

The various aspects of studying the *life sciences* that come into play at this time have been mentioned above. The first main lesson in *zoology* begins with a consideration of the human being. A central aspect of Waldorf education, namely always to relate teaching content to the human being in some way, is evident here. The descriptions of animals and their highly specialized capacities, compared to the unspecialized human being, highlight each animal's specific ability—their highly developed senses, for instance, or their characteristic ways of moving—and their associated highly developed organs (eyes, olfactory lobes, limbs). Thus the picture arises that what distinguishes humanness is precisely its non-specialization, its universality.

In approaching *botany*, Steiner suggests drawing a parallel between the progressive sequence from the lower to the higher plants and the developmental stages of a human life from infant to adolescent. (Steiner 1984: GA 295, p. 128f) What unfolds in the child in terms of a personal emotional and mental life, with which the pupils are familiar from experience, is directly perceptible in the sequence of individual plant forms as a physical image of increasing differentiation and development of new abilities. In addition, this lesson deals with the plant's relationship to its immediate and wider surroundings, to earth (soil structure and quality) and to sun; with the plant's changes of form through the course of the year; and, in bare outline, with the earth's vegetation belts. With these comparisons the two central themes of evolution and ecological thinking are present—in childlike form—as threads running through the study of the life sciences right from the start (cf. Grohmann 1992). In Grade 6, the mineral world becomes the center of attention for the first time in a *geology* main lesson. This can very well be regarded as an aspect of geography, since geology is a kind of counterpart to astronomy.

Studying the life sciences is intended to generate an attitude of conceptual openness, based on flexible concepts. To this end, what is essential is a mode of presentation in which the phenomena selected are characterized as comprehensively as possible, so that not only real encounters take place, but questions also arise. Every genuine desire to understand a subject originates in wonder. Especially in the study of nature, this should never be forgotten.

No subject is as strongly oriented toward causality as *physics,* which also makes its first appearance in Grade 6. Initially, however, the point is not to focus on physical theories and the formation of hypotheses, but on the experience of fundamental physical phenomena in the realms of acoustics, optics, thermodynamics, magnetism, and static electricity.

Not until Grade 7 is the teaching of physics extended to mechanics, and for two reasons: firstly, that mechanics has to do with the force of gravity, and, if abstract models are to be avoided, direct experience of this force is required. For the young person who is undergoing puberty and is therefore vulnerable to these forces, mechanics shows how these same forces can be objectively applied and made useful. Secondly, mechanics is *the* vehicle for learning how to form physical hypotheses. This form of reasoning dominated the physics of the nineteenth century, and thus creates a rational bias that renders any qualitative understanding of the nonmechanical aspects of physics more difficult. What is important here—and this cannot be overemphasized—is that in teaching science, experience must precede knowledge (cf. Buck/v. Mackensen 1990; Holdrege 2013]

Practical subjects in which experience comes via physical work, and learning thus relates to something concrete, also undergo diversification at this stage. ***Gardening***, in which time and space are experienced as realities in the growth of plants, has already been mentioned. This experience has consequences that are expressed in the practical necessities of horticultural processes.

In Grades 4–6, ***handwork*** also undergoes development. The children learn to crochet (which corresponds very neatly with the patterns they do in form drawing), but they also turn their hand to the creation of three-dimensional forms: knitting with five needles to make gloves and socks, for instance, or sewing stuffed animals. Here they must have a clear idea of the finished form in the matter of cutting out the shape (awareness of cause and effect is also part of the picture). At this stage, also, this "lighter" form of crafts moves toward something more "heavy," namely, ***woodworking***,[19] in which again both boys and girls participate.

Working with wood is an object lesson in the meaning of consistency. The pupils are shown that wood and tools, if brought together in the right way, form a unity. In sawing, carving, planing, and sanding, this same lesson applies. Whereas in handwork, the resistance offered by the material is relatively small (unless it's leather), wood represents a stronger challenge.

A similar motif is to be found in ***sports/gymnastics***. In games the circle becomes a line with a goal—for instance, in relay races. If the challenge is not taken up, nothing is accomplished. The same experience is to be gained through exercises with gymnastics equipment, along with light athletics and swimming.

All of this is reminiscent of the concluding remarks on the horizontal curriculum for Grades I to 3, in which the child's need to feel

---

19 On the prelude to crafts work, see the more detailed "vertical" description of the grade school curriculum in Part III of this work, available only online in this English-language translation.

in possession of new abilities was singled out as an essential learning motif. To support the child in this feeling is crucial, because it lays the foundations for further development.

In the continuation of the *story material* in Grades 4 to 6, new motifs appear each year. Fourth graders still live in the mytho-poetic realm of archetypal stories, such as is represented in the sagas of Norse mythology. By fifth grade, historical stories arise not from the gods but from the interaction of gods and humans on earth, and by sixth through eighth grades these stories become focused on the struggles and triumphs of human beings among themselves.

In this way curiosity, interest, and the desire to know are all aroused, and the will to learn is encouraged.

Summary

During the phases of development in which the child becomes detached from his or her surroundings, it is extremely important that a connection to the world is established on a deeper level and strengthened through coherently presented and diverse experiences. To be able to perform useful work in the world (which specific subjects in the curriculum make possible) helps the child discover what it means to take on responsibility. At the heart of such a positive attitude to the world is a feeling, not of resignation, but of readiness for action.

GRADES 7 AND 8

At the beginning of puberty, roughly between the ages of twelve and fourteen, the young person enters into a new relationship to the world. The second growth spurt, which primarily manifests in a remarkable increase in the length of limbs, is not only a physical phenomenon but also involves a corresponding increase in mental capacity.

"There is, therefore, a pedagogical need to understand that in the middle of childhood the child establishes *his or her own timing* of the rhythm between known past and anticipated future."

(Müller-Wiedemann 1999, p. 119) This future, which the young person already senses, has an "existential tinge" (op. cit.) to it. By the same token, the adolescent feels unique while at the same time wishing to belong to a like-minded group. This polarity is captured in Steiner's concept of "earthly maturity." (cf. Steiner: GA 317, p. 18)

The faculty of conceptual thinking developing at this age is oriented toward establishing connections between individual phenomena. And this correlative thinking, which leads to the forming of judgments, requires—Steiner strongly emphasises this point—enhanced imagination. We must not neglect "to bring imagination continually into the power of judgment that slowly approaches at the age of 12." (Steiner: GA 293, p. 200)

A subject that appears for the first time in Grade 7 is *chemistry*, which is intended to acquaint the students with the world of the elements. The phenomenological method of teaching entails a step-wise approach to the forming of concepts, rather than starting with axiomatic definition. The intention of the first step in the apprehension of "objective reality" is to engage the young person with all of his or her senses. "All experience must be lifted into the realm of primal thinking; otherwise it becomes stunted and only generates a craving for sensation. It's not a question of cultivating hard scientific knowledge, but of nurturing the basic motif of science in action: correlative thinking." (Buck/von Mackensen 1990, p. 22)

The main lesson begins with an introduction to chemical processes, in which fire in its various manifestations figures prominently (an experience close to the hearts of young people at this age!). This opens the way to understanding the variety of substances. Here due attention should also be paid to aspects of cultural and technological history associated with the mastery and uses of fire.

In Grade 8, this subject is mainly concerned with the chemistry of food. The study of these organic processes has two sides: the human being removes food from its natural context; connection is restored when the food is eaten. The object of the main lesson is to discern the characteristic qualities of foodstuffs as they appear in the products of nature. Here the pupils are asked to discover the origin of various foods by doing their own experiments. This subject becomes purely scientific in tone later in Grade 9.

The thematic emphasis in Grade 7 *physics* is mechanics, something "inert" but at the same time a stimulus to the imagination. This topic has two main strands: on the one hand, it meets the desire for knowledge of the practical organization of the world, as found in commerce, industry, and transport ("relevance for everyday life"); on the other hand, the students also have the opportunity to try out things for themselves, to "play" with mechanical experiments, make their own discoveries, and, thus, in seeking to take things further, arrive at questions of scientific method. In this way they learn how to test and bring order to their thinking. How mechanics expands into other areas of physics, or supplies a tool for understanding them (e.g. hydraulics, aeronautics, etc.) is taken up in Grades 8 and 9. As before, the use of abstract models is avoided, but in specific places—Grade 7 mechanics is well suited for this—a start is made on quantitative method and the use of formulae (e.g. "the golden rule of mechanics"). As mentioned above, it should become clear to the students just how relevant the lesson content is to the everyday operations of industry and their attendant social consequences.

Building upon the more systematic survey of Grade 6, *geography* in Grade 7 now concerns itself with specific areas of the earth not yet considered in detail. Their special features, unique cultural conditions, and combination of peoples are the center of attention. Looking at different countries and cultures leads young people to the theme of individuation, just at a time when they themselves are busy with the question of their own developing individuality. Correlation and imagination: in this lesson both these abilities are fully exercised when, in connection with different parts of the earth, metamorphosis—via polarity and intensification, as Goethe famously phrased it—becomes the subject of study.

In *life sciences* the human being now becomes the central focus. As a topic for Grade 7 Steiner suggests dealing with questions of health and nutrition. His reasoning behind this is that Grade 7 is the last time the human being can be presented in a way that is free of egotism, because human nature is still experienced in a generalized manner. (Steiner 1990: GA 294, p. 186f.)[20] One can combine this with gardening: medicinal plants, organic food growing, etc., as well as human reproduction and sexuality. In Grade 8 the focus on human biology continues under the rubric of "earthly maturity." The organs whose functions are most closely connected to the outside world—the sense organs and those associated with movement (the skeleton and the voluntary muscles)—are the objects of study. This topic gives young people direct personal experience of their own body's dealing with the force of gravity.

If the lesson just described was about "discovering the human being," *history* in Grade 7 is about the discovery and exploration of new continents, and the discovery of natural laws in both science and art (e.g. perspective). As regards the "discovery" of new continents, this could very fruitfully be considered from the perspective of the cultures thus encountered. The beginning of the triumphant march of scientific thinking in the Renaissance, as well as the growth of individualism in relation to the world-view and belief system hitherto regarded as valid, both represent a very clear parallel to the dynamics of the developmental stage the students have reached at this time.

The coming of industrialization, the Industrial Revolution, and the human being as the architect of various kinds of social order right up to the present time are all themes certain to engage the thoughts and feelings of Grade 8 students. Questions about a more just, humane, and ecologically responsible social and economic order are also sure to arise in discussion. Thus, by becoming aware through cultural history of the transformation of the world through human influence, and

---

20 For an account of how nutrition and everything connected with it can, from Grade 1 on, gradually be molded into a subject in its own right, see the online Part III of this guide.)

in practicing causal observation and thinking in their science lessons, a lively interest "in all worldly and human matters" arises in the students. (cf. Steiner 1984: GA 295, p. 166.)

The discovery of the vanishing point at the time of the Renaissance provides the basic theme for *drawing and painting (art)*. Exercises and studies in perspective based on works by great masters constitute a challenge to create pictorial art geometrically. Once students have grasped the technique and also become acquainted with color perspective, the attempt can be made to turn the content of a black-and-white work—i.e., its inner mood—into color. This is not just a coloring-in exercise; what is meant is a color conversion that adequately captures an intense engagement with the picture's graphic qualities.

An appreciation of the meaning of what has just been called "inner mood" can be introduced or supported by *language arts*, or native language lessons in Grade 7. On the program are, among other things, interjections, which are of course nothing less than expressions of feeling. The idea is that the students learn to recognize them and turn them into other forms of expression. At a time when young people are likely to have become somewhat inarticulate as they search for their own individual voice, this subject can offer significant help, perhaps by purposefully cultivating both choral and individual speaking of verse and prose. Many schools include a main lesson on creative writing entitled "Wish, Wonder, and Surprise."

In connection with "seeking a voice," the study of different types of sentences can be repeated in a completely new way in Grade 8. This can then lead to investigation of questions such as how the sentence structure of certain passages reveals the predominance of a particular temperament. Sanguine, melancholic, choleric, phlegmatic—once the students become aware of these character traits they begin to see (and often appreciate) each other in new ways. In the study of ballads, they further begin to wake up to their own literary preferences. This then leads to questions of style and to the discovery of the distinctive features of epic and lyric poetry. Here, special attention should be paid to nonliteral, pictorial rhetorical figures like metaphor, simile, synecdoche, and others. A noticeable gain in "self-knowledge" can also be effected by a short excursion into philosophical language (Herder, say, or Emerson; cf. Dühnfort/Oltmann 1989).

Then there is drama, a central motif of this age group. Here just reading or reciting a ballad will not do: rather, what is required is the mounting of a major theater project—the class play! In approaching such a work of dramatic art, the social element is of essential importance, and the opportunity to forge social cohesion should be exploited to the hilt.

Foreign or world languages can be treated in a similar vein. By composing their own reports and stories, the students are doing the same kinds of exercises as those described above. In learning about the geography, history, people, and culture of the countries associated with particular languages, it is important to place all this within the context of the universally human: "What I have said, however, about the characteristics of various languages means that it is actually necessary—if we wish to give people of today a genuinely human, as opposed to a one-sidedly chauvinistic education and upbringing—to view language in such a way that whatever emerges about human nature from the genius of the one language must be balanced by something from the other language" (Steiner 1986: GA 307, p. 200).

In this connection the ***story material*** for this age may be mentioned in passing. Anything is appropriate that creates interest in peoples from all the far-flung corners of the earth. This helps foster cross-cultural understanding and, of course, has a close relationship to geography.

The topic for ***astronomy*** is the replacement of the world-view *experienced* as geocentric by one *conceived* as heliocentric, a dramatic change of perspective. Here there is a clear connection to the teaching of history (Copernicus, Galileo, Kepler). In relation to the Age of Discovery, the basic principles of nautical navigation can also be discussed.

Grade 8 *mathematics*, like physics, sees the wholesale introduction of formulae. Starting from the formula for calculating interest (Grade 6), algebra and the theory of equations are presented. Then, in the extraction of roots, a further mathematical and analytical encounter with the "experience of perspective" occurs: An ever-expanding numerical vista opens up before the students in working with powers, and then beyond the "zero threshold," for the first time, they enter the realm of negative numbers. The previously mentioned capacity for correlative thinking is exercized further in the continuation of commercial computation, for instance with book-keeping. The basic concepts behind this can already be covered in Grade 7. (cf. Brater/Munz 1994, Fucke 1993.)

In *geometry* the emphasis is on practicing the construction of proofs. This involves everything from the congruence of triangles and the theory of Pythagoras to the altitude and cathetus theorems. Constant repetitive practice in drawing and constructing proofs trains judgment and will. Perspective constructions reveal connections with both history and art, while those involving the Golden Section open up a parallel to human biology (Grade 8).

Geometry gives the students the possibility of arriving at exact judgments and concepts, whereas in *music* these are much more nebulous. Nevertheless, in this realm of preeminently inner expression, the students should also be enabled to find their way by forming sound judgments. Thus, they not only become acquainted with different composers and musical styles but can also develop an understanding for the process of composition—in other words, for musical "translation."

As before, instrumental music and singing, especially as aids to social cohesion, are still given as much attention as listening. Like eurythmy, music is particularly well suited to prevent young people from getting lost in their growing feelings of isolation by keeping them in contact with each other.

In *eurythmy* the program includes ballads and humoresques. This aspect of the eurythmy curriculum represents a support, an "interpretational aid" for lessons in language arts or one's native language, while tone-eurythmy offers a useful complement to music. In a lecture for the first Waldorf teachers, Steiner describes the significance of eurythmy for the development of the fundamental principle of social life, namely, the ability to listen: "So you are always engaged in eurythmy when you listen [....] The manifestation of the activity of the listener is, in fact, eurythmy. [...] People cannot listen and will become increasingly less able to do so in these times, unless the power of listening is stirred to life afresh by eurythmy [....] People will have to learn to respect one another before socialization can begin. They can only do this if they really listen to each other." (Steiner 1990: GA 294, p. 61f.)

In connection with language arts lessons, the *class play* of Grade eight has already been mentioned. Preparing and carrying through such an undertaking means working on a scale very much larger than the plays and scenes that have been an integral part of lessons from Grade 1 on. In the class play, there is for the first time the opportunity to express aspects of soul life—still behind the protective mask of a role—which reveal the motives and impulses of human characters. Through the combination of working on sets (painting and carpentry), sewing costumes (handwork), designing posters (drawing, painting), choreography (eurythmy), and music, a grand synthesis of everything that has been learned so far is created at the end of elementary school. That is one point; the other is that, through the coming together of various arts, a composite or total work of art can come into being. This highlights the need for new kinds of creative ability based on social awareness, as opposed to individual work on the separate arts.

In the section on *handwork* for Grades 1 to 3, the importance of becoming skilled at something was mentioned. This skill now finds its application in activities that make more use of technology, though without in any way neglecting the artistic and aesthetic aspect that has been nurtured from the outset. Once again this presents a challenge to the creative imagination. Thus, the work may be the designing and making of shoes, with attention paid to both what they are for and who is going to wear them. In relation to themes of history, practice is gained in the use of sewing machines, culminating (perhaps in Grade 9) in the production of complicated items such as shirts, blouses, trousers, skirts, and other individually designed clothes.

Crafts offers girls and boys the possibility of designing and constructing items of various kinds, and of turning their hand for the first time to carpentry. Making moving toys depends upon a basic knowledge of mechanics, since the student not only needs to understand the mechanics of the particular piece, but is also responsible for designing it. Household objects carved by hand (bowls, boxes with lids, nutcrackers etc.) should not just be functional, but should meet certain artistic criteria. In their design they should combine function with beauty of form, in true "arts and crafts" style. In joinery a special challenge lies in working accurately enough to achieve a perfect fit.

At some point there should come a moment of stretching oneself beyond one's own personal limits, one's comfort zone. Especially in ***gardening*** the significance of this is not to be underestimated: indolence, say, or antipathy, is addressed by this activity. Simply having to accept changes in the weather while working outdoors can be a real challenge for the students. The idea is to get practical experience of as much of the horticultural year as possible: from sowing and rearing seedlings to transplanting, watering, hoeing, weeding, and harvesting. Then come the processing and perhaps the selling of the produce. Partaking actively in this cycle schools the sense of personal responsibility. In the care of shrubs and trees this is even more strongly the case, for they require forethought that spans years. Gardening is thus a future-oriented subject, through which the students develop a real sense of what sustainability means.

Pushing oneself beyond personal limits and the measure of self-awareness that goes with it also come to the fore in ***gymnastics***. For this reason the focus is on exercises using gymnastics equipment, as well as jumping in its manifold forms. Practice in endurance is also continued with an intensive training in running. In addition to thus nurturing individual development, it is also essential to develop social abilities through team sports and games. With the onset of puberty, a separation of the sexes may be introduced into gym lessons.

As with the class play, there is an opportunity in Grade 8 to carry out an individual practical/artistic/social ***project*** over the course of the year. Its themes and methods are diverse; the common aim, however, is for the students to test their ability to do their own work, and to structure, document, and present it. (In doing this, many will once again come up against the need to step out of their comfort zone.) At a time when it is often difficult to reach young people, to "meet" them, a project like this offers a chance for a new kind of individual contact, based on something concrete.

Summary

By the time they complete their education in the elementary grades of a Waldorf school, children can expect to have

- been introduced to the laws of nature

- found their own voice in dialogue and confrontation, in which the imagination is always challenged

- experienced how knowledge facilitates well-founded judgments

- formed judgments to bring new questions to light

- begun to feel they belong in the world, on the earth

CHAPTER 4

BACKGROUND TO TEACHING IN THE HIGH-SCHOOL GRADES

Adolescence can be regarded as a developmental phase that starts with the advent of puberty, or "earthly maturity," and culminates with the attainment of majority. During this time, teenagers live within the tension between a process unfolding along predetermined lines and a growing sense of freedom. Every young person swings between these extremes in an entirely unique way. It is a particularly striking expression of the nature of a developmental transition: It announces itself in both mental and physical terms, most dramatically in an unmistakable physiological process, which forces the adolescent into a new relationship to his or her own bodily make-up.

The inner aspect of this maturation process now sets the young person tasks, such as the need to develop self-awareness, self-control, and the ability to form relationships. All of this requires pedagogical support. Steiner sums up this whole process as a "new, third birth"—that of the soul (also known as astral) body. (The first birth is the process we normally designate as birth, the beginning of the life path. The second is marked by the change of teeth around the age of seven: at this time of transition, the forming and transforming of the body's organs attains a degree of completion, such that the transformative agents become more readily available for the purposes of memory and thinking.(cf. Steiner 1987: GA 34, p. 321–323)

Before this "third birth," feelings were the source of a half-conscious inner life. Now they take on a much more existential quality as the fundamental currency of personal experience, upon which a new level of independence is based. The inner now seeks to meet the outer much more through conscious intention. Relationships with people and the surrounding world are colored largely by judgments. And at this stage of development, around the age of 15, judgments are formed predominantly in connection with ideals and principles. It is plainly evident that the adolescent is driven by a sense of the ideal—in relation to the self, to others, and to the world.

All lesson content should try to meet and satisfy this need in one way or another. To satisfy does not mean to pacify; nothing could be further from the demands of this stage of development than peace and quiet! What is required, rather, is the experience of a demonstrable lawfulness that can be discovered by one's own thinking, and which is revealed as true or based on reliable evidence. There arises the possibility of carrying out what has been discerned as necessary, even when this self-conceived intention goes against one's personal inclinations. Thus the young person can realize the idea of *duty* as something that emanates deep from within oneself, and the feeling of *responsibility* for one's own actions. Personal opinion becomes important, as does finding one's "own voice." Out of this the young person develops his or her own personality. Once this first phase has been successfully navigated and the physical and emotional turmoil it often entails has died down, adolescent development can take a further step.

Around the age of 16 the crisis and drama of puberty begins to subside. The proportions of the body once more become harmonious. The inclination toward serious work becomes stronger, although this seriousness stands in danger of becoming eccentric: "The adolescent, in all modesty, assigns himself a decisive role in saving humanity and plans his life accordingly." (Piaget 1974, p. 3) Here the teacher can and should help by providing exemplary materials as a basis for forming judgments. The young person needs to learn that judging means being true to the phenomenon. A confrontation—sometimes disillusioning—with the limits of reality may ensue, which is why Steiner recommends approaching the formation of judgments through facts, causality, order, and the perception of phenomena in relation to one another. Security and confidence can then be built on a relationship to the world, based soundly upon clear thinking.

The other side of the painful process of coming to terms with limits is to explore and question them. This is why it is important to investigate and discuss how far the interpretation of judgments and theories can be extended. Behind this also stands the experience of the finite nature of one's own existence, from which can emerge the realization: I could opt out of my idealist position, and in so doing opt for life as it is.

What is discovered in the course of such ruminations seldom meets ideal expectations, and a teenager's ensuing comments are correspondingly trenchant and mercilessly critical. The young person can thus easily become a skeptic. It is important that science, as presented by the teacher, should appear as a coherent approach to the acquisition of knowledge. Epistemological pessimism is not conducive to the inner well-being of students at this age, although it is very likely to make itself heard in their own words. When this happens, it is actually a challenge to the adult: Well, then, show me that it is not so. "Adolescence, in an entirely objective sense, is overshadowed by tragedy: that of only very seldom finding a living example of what it seeks—the fully self-determined adult." (Fucke 1993, p. 49)

At this time school—as an institution separated from social realities—will not be accepted if it is felt to be out of touch with life. Its responsibility is to assess the available options and offer some options that lead to a secure sense of orientation in the "here and now." Here, of course, young people will unmask anything that smacks of pseudomodernity or mere spectacle. The search for the unattainable ideal now takes shape as the search for authenticity and truth. The teacher's task, then, is to be the medium of positive experiences, for failing this the young person may not find his way toward "grounding his existence in something that gives his life stability and direction *sub specie aeternitatis*. He remains empty; lost in the stream of time." (Fischer 1966, p. 158)

Around the age of 17 a further upheaval takes place, in which a feeling of selfhood shifts much more to the fore. Associated with this is a phase of quietly taking stock of things. Out of all this, the ability to handle multiple points of view begins to emerge. This involves balancing ideas and reality in the dynamics between personal subjectivity and a wider objective context, while respecting other standpoints and levels. Judgments can now lead to a variety of outcomes through processes of dialectical discussion. Because the individual standpoint is developed from the dynamics of the relationship between self and world, it now becomes possible for the first time to open up aesthetic phenomena to real critical appraisal. Empathy, in other words, the possibility of applying emotional intelligence or of experiencing another self as if it were one's own, can become an integral part of classroom culture. On the basis of such a potent experience of selfhood, attention turns toward its future and the young person becomes aware of his or her own biography.

Education that is concerned with such questions—ultimately questions of destiny—can never be value-free. If formerly the teacher's task was to select, evaluate, and present teaching material, he or she must now be experienced as someone on a quest, a researcher in pursuit of his or her own questions. What will inspire the students is not so much the results as the processes by which this person gained insight and developed them. Teachers who are themselves still learners are best suited to inspire the rising generation.

> "[…] our task is not to transmit our convictions to the rising generation. We should lead them to use their own power of judgment, their own intelligence. They should

learn to look at the world with open eyes. Whether or not we personally doubt the truth of what we bring to young people is not the point. Our convictions only matter to us. We offer them to our youth in order to say: this is how we see the world; make sure you find out how you see it. Our job is to awaken *abilities*, not to deliver convictions. The young generation should not believe in our 'truths', but in our personality. That we are *seekers* is what they should perceive in us. And we should guide them onto *the seeker's path*."

(Steiner 1989: GA 31, p. 233f.)

At 18 the students have reached the age of legal adulthood with full voting rights and as such have become socially responsible for their own actions. Accordingly, lessons are much more consciously focused on ethical issues, which entail, among other things, comprehensive thinking, self-reflection, and self-motivation. Now it becomes essential to consider the interrelationships among various subjects and areas of knowledge, their cultural and scientific significance, and their implications for the understanding of human nature. Above all, in the process of forming judgments, the important thing is to be aware of one's own assumptions. More emphatically than before, knowledge gained from any subject can be seen as a contribution toward a better understanding of the human being.

At the end of Grade 12—or, as the case may be, after Grade 13—the third seven-year phase of life is far from over. The last portion of this phase, however, will not be spent in high school. The desire is now to see the world, go into further education, learn a trade or profession. What to aim for in life becomes clearer. When the fulfillment of these aims is delayed by circumstances, such as a lack of study or training opportunities, this often leads to restlessness, a gradual decline in the will to learn, and other difficulties. For this reason a number of Waldorf schools have developed high-school models incorporating a rich range of practical training opportunities, which have been operating successfully for many years. Here schooling does not culminate simply in an examination of some kind, but rather in the completion of an apprenticeship or social training of some kind. Thus Waldorf education, by way of honoring its obligation to the individual biography as a whole, is able to combine school-as-institution with preparation for the much larger school of life. Which of its many paths and options to follow is then up to the freedom of the individual, in whom the Self, the "'I' as the kernel of the soul" (Steiner 2003: GA 9, p. 60), is now becoming awake and active.

A young person prepared in this way will be able to take his or her place in the world as a free and responsible individual, and thereby make a personal contribution to the future development of society.

In terms of educational practice this implies that the schooling of intellectual capacity goes hand-in-glove with character building and the cultivation of imagination. Artistic and practical activities are therefore regarded as equal in value to the cognitive transmission of factual knowledge; they should, in fact, interpenetrate one another. Being well educated is not achieved by training the intellect alone, but is the result of a holistic process. Pedagogy should not restrict itself to dealing just with specific subject matter; it must address the whole person. Only when education manages to develop intellect, feeling, and will in equal measure, and to communicate and exemplify freedom, equality, and brotherhood, can it be described as "successful."

People who have been through such a process will not shirk the challenges of life, will not give up in the face of crisis; rather they will help to make sense of things, find new ways of doing things, and also be the ones to undertake them. Thus, the design of every lesson becomes an instance of the "art of education," for the teaching method generally is artistic work and in its practical realization is the living expression of a creative personality engaged in self-development. At the same time the whole process is a question of timing: the right material in the right form at the right time.

If the teacher is able to work through and understand the laws of development—something that is required of every Waldorf teacher—he or she will have acquired the ability to "read" the human being. The specific physiological and psychological phenomena that appear in the course of human maturation are like letters of the alphabet waiting to be placed into a meaningful context. ("Meaningful" is not meant as the interpretation of a momentary state, but refers to the ability to grasp the nature of the human being as a whole. Here comparison with the plant may be permitted: its totality can only be conceived by contemplation of the overall sequence of its phases of growth.)

If this "reading the essence of the human" (Steiner 1986: GA 308, p. 47) leads to pedagogical actions that further the overall well-being of the growing human individual, then a teacher can be said to have developed educational competence. "Insofar as it falls under the jurisdiction of school, he can take on full educational responsibility [....] Knowledge of the human being, however, only becomes practically useful in the hands of the individual teacher. The curriculum for him, then, is not a prescribed course of action, for it comes into being for him on the basis of the developmental conditions of a particular age group." (Kranich 1990, p. 98)

CHAPTER 5

HORIZONTAL CURRICULUM OF THE HIGH-SCHOOL YEARS

GRADE 9

In *history* the focus is on modern times, with the aim of acquainting the students with the leading ideas of this epoch and thus awakening in them an understanding of the present. This can be done in connection with historical processes and events of particular relevance to the prevailing culture. Grand ideas and ideals were the impulse behind major historical upheavals, such as the French Revolution or the American War for Independence. These examples highlight a problem which is exactly the one facing young people of this age, namely that on the path from the conception to the realization of an ideal, reality must be included and recognized; in other words, that violence and collapse can be a consequence of moral rigidity. The last "blank spots" on the globe now disappear for the students; their awareness begins to encompass the earth and humanity as a whole. The job of the history main lesson(s) is to awaken interest in world affairs. Here it is important to lead young people into the processes of forming their own judgments. They should also delve into the workings of historical transformations by investigating the significance of historical figures who championed certain ideas.

The theme of the attainment of human and civil rights based upon such values as freedom, equality, and solidarity that arose in history can be covered in more depth and detail in a main lesson on *social studies*. This involves learning about processes of political decision-making and the formation of public opinion (parliament, political parties, the press). Awakening an active interest in world affairs is a key element of this whole school year and affects the teaching of all subjects. Through hearing the biographies of prominent figures, students may conceive ideas for their own future. This also helps to refine their feeling for the intrinsic worth of ideals in contrast to the experience of injustice or sympathy for the oppressed. The students are familiarized with various ways of participating in the political process, the structure and function of governmental institutions, and also the various judicial pathways open to them (the structure of the legal system).

In *physics,* the topics are thermodynamics in relation to key examples of human inventions in these areas. The students begin by getting hands-on experience of the rationally designed technology of the 18th and 19th centuries (steam engine, locomotive, internal combustion engine, electric motor, telephone). The further developments of these achievements can then be followed right up to the present. The crucial thing here is for the students to get to know the people, ideas, and intentions behind the inventions. In this way they can see how it is possible to construe technology as "externalized human thoughts," and a glimpse into the workshop of such thought processes, as well as into the biography of their inventor, creates an impression that is warm and inspiring, unburdened by any kind of moralizing or cultural pessimism.

In *mathematics,* the central topic is combinatorial analysis (permutations and combinations), extending all the way to calculations of probability; this gives plenty of scope for engaging the power of independent logical thinking, which is just awakening. Many kinds of procedures involving sequence and series (for instance, the Fibonacci Series) as well as calculations of area and volume are performed.

Geometry is concerned with regular bodies such as the Platonic solids. First, the attempt is made to visualize the processes involved in their construction; simple models are then constructed. The procedure with conic sections is similar, and this marks the dramatic advance over Grade 8: starting from dynamic visualizations, the ellipse, parabola, and hyperbola can be developed.

Biology covers the same terrain as the topics raised in Grade 8 life science main lessons: namely, the human sense organs, skeleton, and musculature. The point here is to highlight the drastic change in method: while the class teacher brought these topics in a way that stayed close to the concrete experience of life, the high school teacher now has the job of demonstrating the abundance of new insights that flow from more exact anatomical and functional analysis and synthesis. The power of discernment requires sustenance: science in the best sense now begins. Good communication between class teachers and high-school teachers is essential.

Geology begins to turn the students' gaze toward the earth as a whole, and in Grade 9 the focus is on the earth's mantle. At this stage the student's awakening personality is beginning to take shape but is still uneven; the associated power of judgment has strengthened, and is now brought to bear upon geological phenomena. Through a factual understanding of the physical basis of our existence as it appears in geomorphological processes (continental drift, plate tectonics, volcanism, uplift, and subduction), the students gain a more conscious relationship to them.

In ***chemistry*** the students discover how chemical substances form: combustion and carbonization of products, the decay of organic compounds up to and including humus formation, the origin of crude oil, chemical transformation processes in plants. In distillation (of alcohol) they experience alternating volatility and condensation, filtration, and purification: in other words, processes they are experiencing within themselves.

Art, which first begins as a subject in its own right in the high school, is of central significance for the Grade 9 year. Its task is to provide a counterbalance to the weightiness of the scientific subjects with their strict objective laws, and show the students a world where order created by the human imagination is the determining factor. Through encounters with great masterpieces of sculpture and painting, students develop an enthusiastic appreciation of art and come to the realization that, in pursuing artistic work, the human being enters a realm of freedom.

Drawing is devoted exclusively to working with light and shadow, black and white, which corresponds exactly to the polarity in which the ninth grader is living.

In ***language arts and literature,*** there are two main areas that can be covered. In one main lesson block the students are concerned with the lives and ideas of certain leading figures of classical literature. In this connection the theme of friendship naturally arises (for instance, that between Goethe and Schiller, or comparable friendships in the context of other languages and literatures). This is something that touches upon changes that may be occurring in the class community and in the students' lives in general. The theme of the other main lesson is humor and tragedy. Humor, at least in the form of wit, creates detachment. For a group of young people going through puberty, it is perhaps useful to have this piece of worldly wisdom brought home to them in a variety of ways, especially through literary examples. Moreover, criticism—including self-criticism—is toned down to a bearable level in the light of humor. Laughter is an expression of feeling whereby the human individual seeks to come to terms with an apparent incongruity. Of course, there are also ways of expressing polar opposite feelings of tragedy, such as sympathy, pity, and sorrow, and these should figure equally in the lesson. Through the aesthetic experience of these two sides of the soul, the Grade 9 student gains an impression of how things in general are both polarized and potentially connected. The grammatical aspect of this work consists in developing a grasp, in theory and practice, of a range of literary stylistic devices and forms.

In the process of distancing themselves from their surroundings, adolescents tend to do the same with their mother tongue. This can result in the creation of slang in which expressions from a foreign language, or the language of their own subculture often drawn from internet slang, are adopted. This inclination toward alienation from one's own language can be an advantage for ***foreign language*** teaching, which can also work effectively against the decline of language usually associated with this alienation. A grand, systematic review of grammar is undertaken; possibilities for new understanding open up for all material previously learned mostly through oral exercises. The students encounter ways of thinking that are uncommon in their native tongue: their newfound detachment becomes a source of fun. As reading material, biographies of scientists, inventors, and great figures of the times being studied in history can be selected. Such role models can be of help to young people in shaping their own ideals and future aims.

Music takes a similar approach. The biographies of great musicians are studied as a way of kindling interest in their works. There is a ready receptivity at this age for anything to do with transformation or metamorphosis, and this, enhanced by artistic experience, can help the young person come to terms with his or her own "process of reconstruction." Hence, the main idea here is that the students be taken inside the experience of how one style of music turns into another. This could be done in a European context by taking works by Baroque composers—say, Händel and Bach—and comparing (and contrasting) them with works from the Classical era, such as Mozart and early Beethoven; but such representative transformational processes could also be found in other historical and cultural contexts. By trying out some of these examples—and they need to be worthy of the attention paid them—both vocally and possibly instrumentally, the students experience the music not just emotionally, but also in terms of the "grammar" of its musical language, and they also develop the ability to hear and reproduce modifications of melodic structures. From Grade 9 on it is desirable for students to take part in musical ensembles of some kind: choir, orchestra, etc.

In *eurythmy,* poems and compositions from the period being studied in history, chosen for their particular appropriateness for this age group, are transposed into movement and form, very simply and without frills. The students should be aware of what artistic elements are being employed. Humor and athletic movement are essential ingredients at this age.

For *gardening,* there are two main possibilities this year. Either gardening is done in a main lesson block long enough to accommodate landscaping processes, such as the creation of paths, walls, steps, fences, etc.; or it takes the form of an agricultural practicum for two or three weeks during which the students live on a family farm and work in the fields and farmyard. Besides discovering much that is new, they have the chance to experience the stark realities of nature as the regulator of daily life.

In *woodwork,* the students learn how to make simple joins. **Textile work** involves dressmaking and tailoring from patterns they design (dresses, jackets, etc.). In *copper-bashing, iron forging* (sometimes not until Grade 10) and *basket-weaving,* similarly shaped artifacts—bowls, cups, and various kinds of baskets—are made in very different ways. By sustained effort, a contained space is fashioned from the periphery inwards.

By following the cross-disciplinary intentions of the curriculum, the educational aims contained within the developmental insights associated with this age can be clearly discerned.

The intentions underlying the Grade 9 year

Teaching is geared toward:

- giving structure to thinking; developing the intellect; using simple causal logic in drawing conclusions; moving from affective (Grade 8) to rational judgment

- interacting with clear, well-structured, easily grasped lesson content; from discovery (Grades 7/8) to invention; analytical approach to whole contexts

- developing interest in world affairs; amassing factual knowledge; introducing technology as a human-made element and as "externalized human thoughts;" studying the human being as culture-maker; experiencing the many-sidedness of the world (cf. Schirmer 1993, p. 165)

- becoming familiar with particular ideas and ideals, as well as forming judgments in connection with them; gaining personal inspiration from hearing about the struggles of exemplary human beings in their attempts to realize the ideals of modern humanity

GRADE 10

In everything they do in Grade 10, the students' individual personalities come much more to the fore. Ways should therefore be found to encourage self-motivation and self-discovery, initially in the realm of thinking. Clarity in thinking and increasing powers of discernment should help the adolescent free him- or herself from the arbitrary tangles of antipathy and sympathy. A main concern, then, is to cultivate thinking by approaching the discovery of patterns and laws in an analytical way.

Steiner's curricular indications of 17/6/1921 for ***biology*** are as follows: "Create an understanding for the human being as a single organism [....] The physical human organism in the form and function of its organs in relationship to the activities of soul and spirit." (Steiner 1924: GA 300b, p. 27) This is best begun by means of a morphological approach, to which physiological and psychosomatic aspects of organ function can then be added step by step. For adolescents, this opens up an area in which there is an ongoing interplay of those very developmental processes in which they themselves are embroiled. For the whole period of puberty, with its outer and inner changes—basically from Grade 7 to Grade 10—the plant and animal worlds are dealt with in gardening lessons and in the agricultural practicum, while the main lessons are exclusively devoted to human biology. This is clearly intended to help the rising generation arrive at a new relationship to their own physical nature.

In *earth science* the comprehensive approach already begun now extends to the hydrosphere and atmosphere, including the earth's climatic zones and yet other spheres (from the depths of the earth to the zones beyond the stratosphere). This involves consideration of their movements and complex interactions, while *astronomical* aspects can also be taken into account. All this is a further contribution to building up a basis for understanding the biosphere and its ecology. The aim is to arrive at a view of the earth as a living organism that reacts very sensitively to disturbances of its rhythms and cycles.

If *gardening* is offered in Grade 10, the theme is one that figures large in the shaping of human cultures: namely, the grafting of fruit trees and shrubs such as roses. Just as the agricultural practicum can be a special form of "gardening" in Grade 9, so here it can take the form of a *forestry practicum*.

In *history,* the foreground is occupied by a topic which clearly relates to both geography and gardening: the interaction of human cultural development with topographical and climatic conditions. An understanding of nomadic hunter-gatherers and the formation of settlements (Neolithic revolution), as well as the special features of the cultures of Egypt, Mesopotamia, and Greece, should be developed from their respective geographical backgrounds. According to the particular cultural context, another sequence of cultures could be chosen. Here also the connection between the human being and the earth is very evident, and, beyond that, the development of humanity as a process of gradual emancipation from blood ties toward free individuality.

In Grade 10 there is also a clear shift of emphasis in *social studies,* which parallels that in history. Attention is now directed toward the conditions that apply to all human beings equally. This opens up a field of study that involves coming to an understanding of laws, principles, and bills of rights. It also entails consideration of the material and natural conditions behind all economic activity and the basic forms of society that arise from it. The founding of a civilization through the establishment of a constitutional state, as well as an introduction to the basic elements of professional and economic life and their dependence upon geographical and cultural circumstances, are themes by which *social studies* gives support to adolescents in the search for their own place in the world. Numerous cross-connections to geography, gardening, and history can be made here.

The *language* main lesson block takes a similar approach. If it is **German** it will be concerned with Norse mythology, based on extracts from the Edda, the Icelandic Sagas, and the Song of Hildebrand, as well as examples of medieval poetry. This charts a course where the students can experience the breakup of old ancestral ties and a concomitant emergence of a spirit of individual responsibility. In the case of other native languages and cultures, other mythologies, such as the stories of Gilgamesh or Beowulf, can be selected to express a corresponding development. Working with the Nibelungenlied (and possibly with other epics) gives the opportunity to deal with a number of themes; for instance, how a form of action bound to tribal values, which leads to disaster, could be viewed in terms of current ethics, which opens up possibilities of how the catastrophe could have been avoided.

A main lesson like this offers the possibility of branching out into other areas of the same educational terrain. Starting from Middle-High German, one could awaken awareness of language as something constantly in process of change by considering historical shifts in the sounds and meanings of words. A further point of emphasis could consist in opening up the world of drama by comparing an ancient with a modern play. This would, at the same time, constitute a study in poetics. In English-speaking schools, the focus of this main lesson is more likely to be the unique twin Latin and Anglo-Saxon ancestry of modern English.

The focus of **arts** shifts to poetics, or the structure of poetry. In this way, one of the "time arts" takes its place among the arts of space. The structural principles of poetry—rhythm, sound, image—are investigated using epic, lyric, and dramatic examples, with ample opportunity for associated creative writing exercises.

Eurythmy also concentrates on the technicalities of poetry, and the features peculiar to each type are brought to expression by groups moving in concert. At this stage, the students also create their own forms.

In *foreign language lessons,* the intention is to make a first approach to the understanding of style. Unabridged literature is increasingly used. This creates the possibility of getting a feeling for another cultural milieu and coming to appreciate other ways of thinking. Coming to grips with the use of tenses for a variety of specific purposes demands exact thinking. Stating a case and justifying it in the foreign language encourages the ability to think in that language.

In *music,* the students acquire the principles for understanding a wide range of compositions. Practical experience is gained from singing in the choir and playing in the orchestra. In connection with what has been learned in this way, harmony theory is expanded on the basis of further examples.

The main lessons in mathematics, physics, chemistry, geometry, land surveying, and stellar navigation are all similar in approach. In the content of *physics,* the educational principle of the Grade 10 year appears particularly clearly. Nowhere are the laws of nature so straightforward and so easy to grasp in their derivation as in the realm of classical mechanics. Here the students can proceed from experiment to observation and thence to law, formula, and calculation without anything vague or incomprehensible arising. Clear observation, logic, the construction of causal relationships, and analytical thinking are all schooled. The aim of the lesson is to bring out the connection between theory and practice.

Land surveying—scheduled either as a main lesson or extended practicum offsite—offers the challenge of encountering the topological features of a particular place by means of measurement, technical drawing, and math. The students gain a basic understanding both of the use of equipment and of cartographic conversion, and they sharpen their accuracy skills in the process. Here there are parallels to both geography and cultural history, where one of the topics was methods of land measurement in ancient civilizations (Mesopotamia and Egypt). Most immediately connected to this course, however, is the content of the **mathematics main lesson** concerned with trigonometry, which finds its practical application in land surveying. The cosine theorem is also helpful in physics for the calculation of statics.

Further progress in the explanation of mathematical laws can be achieved in the realm of numerical patterns, powers, and logarithms. As far as possible in this school year, mathematics should have some connection to the practicalities of life.

In *chemistry,* the focus is on the acid-base polarity—now taught not so much through the senses of taste as through the abstract calculations of titration—and crystallization processes in salts. This main lesson is directly related to that in **geometry**, which is largely concerned with the graphic representation of regular and irregular solids and their associated laws of symmetry. If anything, chemistry in Grade 10 is about the introduction of the quantitative approach: the nature of chemical bonds, the properties of glazes, the values in chemical formulae, introduction to electro-chemistry, and, as a high point, the numerical ordering of the elements in terms of the Periodic Table.

If the ***technology of textiles*** is offered, the process from fibre to yarn to textile production can be presented and carried out in practice (spinning, weaving). As with land surveying and other practical activities, the artifact itself, in its unassailable objectivity, corrects the student's errors. The main point of emphasis here is whether the things produced are of any real use. In parallel, other technical appliances of everyday life could just as well be discussed, e.g. bicycle gears, flush toilets, and many others.

Information technology can be regarded as a subsidiary of technology. What is required here is guidance into the basics of computers, right down to the functioning of semi-conductors. It is also desirable to reflect upon the use of various kinds of applications and graphics software.

The students' need for worthwhile, practical activities is also accommodated by a course in ***first aid***. To know how to do the right thing at the right time—that creates true confidence!

In ***art***, starting from basic sculptural exercises, the structural potentialities of the convex-concave polarity are explored. If painting is included in Grade 10, experiments are undertaken in transposing black-white motifs into color.

The intentions underlying the Grade 10 year

Teaching is geared toward:

- achieving objectivity and clarity in thinking, thereby laying the foundation for finding one's place in the world; encouraging logical, causal reasoning (rational, conceptual judgment)

- cultivating analytical understanding of laws in nature; through interaction with all that is conceivable in purely material, physical terms, the students become (fully) conscious inhabitants of the earth, with an understanding of the world in its lawfulness—interest is directed toward the external world (cf. Schirmer 1993, p. 165)

- developing in the students a feeling of confidence in their own knowledge: the world is true or, at any rate, comprehensible

- helping students articulate their own limitations and gradually take on more responsibility for their own actions

GRADE 11

Looking at the Grade 11 curriculum, one can see in the individual subjects what is thematically significant from a cross-disciplinary point of view. This appears on three levels: that of culmination, of process, and of renewal. Out of these three, however, there is an ever-present sense of something that reaches beyond the end point into a realm of immense depth and breadth (ultimately into the infinite). "Now foresight (Grade 9, looking around) and hindsight (Grade 10, looking back) are joined by the longing for insight." (Schirmer 1993, p. 165) Through shifts of perspective, in the interplay between idea and matter, the general and the particular, form and content, microcosm and macrocosm, the individual now determines his or her own standpoint. Discussion, dialectical and aesthetic judgments as well as empathic understanding are now encouraged and expected in all subjects.

Something in this vein appears in ***mathematics***, for instance, in working with sequences and progressions, where the unlimited number of single steps is regulated by the concept of a threshold value. It is also clearly apparent in the study of cell theory and microscopy in ***biology,*** or in an ecological practicum. Here a look into the realm of the microscopically small is followed by a glimpse into the macroscopic realm of the whole biosphere. The helpful notion of "involution" (the polar completary gesture to "evolution") might already be familiar to the students from their study of projective geometry.

Chemistry intensifies the work of the previous year with the study of atomic theory. The focus now is on chemical bonds, in which, on the one hand, molecular microprocesses can be demonstrated, but which, on the other hand, can also be viewed in terms of qualitative aspects that are crucial, for instance, in biochemistry. The cognitive challenge is to treat the phenomenological approach from a number of perspectives, and, on this basis, come to appreciate the atomic description as only one way of understanding material reality.

Similar themes can be found in the subject of *physics*. Whereas in Grade 10 the attention was on mechanical forces, the effects of which could be directly observed with the senses, in Grade 11 the concern is with the effects of electromagnetic fields, the phenomenon of radiation, and the theories of the structure of matter. For all their definitive, logical straightforwardness, they are burdened by contradiction, insofar as they point toward an area of reality that is beyond sense perception. Here, there is clearly an overlap between physics and chemistry.

In one of the two **mathematics** main lessons a step is taken beyond the theorems of Euclid into the realm of projective geometry. Here the students are invited to integrate into their thinking a new concept—that of infinity—through learning to work with three "infinitely distant elements": the point-, line-, and plane-at-infinity. These elements correlate with the cultural history and literature main lessons (e.g. Nicholas of Cusa and Wolfram von Eschenbach's *Parzival*). In the theory of oscillations the previous year's trigonometry can be set in motion, and in the process establish the mathematical basis for understanding the wave theory behind all wireless information transmission. And, in the trigonometry of the sphere, the students experience a dramatic step beyond that of the plane. Just like analytical geometry, it combines the arithmetical with the geometrical. Here, as in many other areas of the Grade 11 year, two disciplines hitherto experienced as separate by the students turn out to be intertwined: relationships begin to reveal themselves.

Culmination, process, and renewal are also themes in *history*. It is concerned with the three legacies of the antique world (Greek, Roman, and Jewish cultures) and the historical transformation that arose from them, which expressed itself above all in the development and spread of Christianity. Added to this, in the interests of intercultural understanding, comes a consideration of the interplay between Islamic culture and the European cultures of the Middle Ages. The essential elements of this epoch are process, confrontation, and exchange and the concomitant mutual enrichment of diverse cultures, or cultural streams: pope and emperor, church and state, Christianity and Islam, Augustine's "Theocracy," the dispute over universals, etc.

In *language arts,* a study can be made of the medieval epic "Parzival," as an example of an *Entwicklungsroman* (a novel dealing with the development of a character all the way from childhood to maturity), or of a work of correspondingly epic proportions and developmental content. If nothing suitable is forthcoming, then "Parzival," in translation, may well be found to fit the bill, since its content has a universal quality. Themes such as a sheltered upbringing, the unconscious incurring of guilt, the lure of adventure, the nature of knighthood and courtly culture, leaving home and going out into the world, growing into adulthood are all biographical motifs that can kindle the students' awareness of their own character. The question that Parzival needs to put to Amfortas—"What ails thee?"—expresses the importance of empathy, i.e. of understanding the I-Thou relationship, in the process of self-realization. In a second main lesson, then, motifs from "Parzival" such as development, self-confrontation, etc. can be considered as they appear in the literature of subsequent centuries, right up to the present. In English-language schools, this is the year for a deeper study of Shakespeare—especially *Hamlet*—and the Romantic poets.

In *social studies,* questions are discussed concerning human interrelationships, social responsibility, and the values upon which society and the understanding of human nature are (or should be) based. These lessons give weight to dialectical thinking and debate, taking into account and systematically comparing differing points of view and alternative ways of thinking. The issues involved in the question of how the social underpinnings of our *conditio humana* are philosophically justified can be dealt with through an introduction to political theory, combined with a survey of the thinkers who have influenced our ideas from the Middle Ages to the present. Economic life, today a phenomenon of global dimensions, is also approached as a social process. This immediately introduces the question of consumerism in relation to social responsibility.

In *foreign language* lessons, the main focus is on reading the works of great poets and dramatists. Themes adapted from those followed in native language classes may also be taken up, and there is the possibility of staging a foreign-language play, or a selection of scenes.

For *geography* this year, there are two avenues of approach. On one hand, the students can be led beyond the bounds of what they have hitherto been able to conceive, with an introduction to cartography, which, following ancient tradition, involves using mathematics and graphics to project the globe onto the plane in various ways. *Astronomy* is often now given as a main lesson in its own right, and also takes the imagination beyond the limits of the earth. On the other hand, adolescents in Grade 11 are much more clearly engaged in seeking their own place, their "inner home." An answer to this exploratory gesture is given by considering the economic geography of the earth as a whole, since it raises awareness of an extra "sphere" created by human action. As a carrier of culture and maker of economies, the human being structures and takes control of space, thereby developing an ever more comprehensive spatial awareness.

If *technology* features in Grade 11, the topic that fits this year is "energy and matter." Here, the different kinds of energy production (gas- and coal-fired, nuclear, hydro-electric, wind- and solar-driven power plants) are all studied in technical detail. Attention is also paid to certain unforeseen consequences of energy conversion. Nowhere does the "world we live in" appear so undeniably as a continuum as in the realm of energy. Interconnections to physics and chemistry as well as to ecology are self-evident. The theme of "raw material" leads the students to the craft of paper making and processing, and thence to everything associated with its industrialization (including printing methods and the problem of recycling). It also relates to what they do in bookbinding.

In *information technology,* the step from Grade 10 to Grade 11 lies in coming to understand processes no longer susceptible to sensory observation. This implies the step from hardware to software, using examples of different forms of programming. Further themes considered are the potentials and dangers of social media networks and those arising from linking human beings and machines.

In *arts* lessons, overlapping topics and complementary perspectives come to the fore. Kinships and polarities of various artistic genres lead to comparisons between the visual-sculptural and the musical-poetic. Polar contrary qualities, such as Apollonian–Dionysian and impressionist–expressionist, are taken as leitmotifs. Music (history) can be given a main lesson block by itself, but painting and music lend themselves very well to being integrated into a combined main lesson.

The path from impressionism to expressionism can also be followed in the students' own artistic practice, especially in *painting*. Something similar occurs in *modeling*: Here the attempt is made to give expression to simple emotional gestures or moods (question, answer, conversation, joy, sorrow) in modeled human figures. Thus the students arrive at sculptural knowledge of the "body as mirror of the soul." This also helps the attempt to extract the "objective" from within the "subjective."

Both body and soul are brought into action in *eurythmy*, taking the above-mentioned artistic processes further by working on poetic and musical examples of the Apollonian and the Dionysian, which involves discussing questions of style and encouraging the students to develop their own ideas in this connection. Their familiarity with the process of working out their own movements now opens up the possibility of developing their eurythmy in the direction of performance, even to the point of performing a solo.

In Grade 11 a *social practicum* can be a key feature of the whole school year. For three weeks the students work in clinics, homes, schools for the disabled, and other such institutions. In having to put themselves in the place of others less fortunate than themselves, they experience new facets of the way human life expresses itself.

Alternatively, an *industrial or job-shadowing practicum* can be undertaken in this school year, if that is appropriate in relation to the school's location and social milieu. Here there is, on the one hand, a chance to experience something of the social, organizational, and economic conditions of the world of work and, on the other, the opportunity to explore ideas for a future career.

The intentions underlying the Grade 11 year

Teaching is geared toward:

- developing a capacity for a more objective self-observation no longer at the mercy of one's subjective feelings, thereby increasing powers of discernment and of empathy (ability to judge matters of taste, style, laws of social behavior)

- bringing flexibility and diversification into thinking, and leading the strictly logical, law-bound mentality of the tenth grade into a new dimension

- encouraging contextual thinking (synthesis); process thinking that points beyond a single cause (relationships involving variable causes, reciprocal processes) and derives its own standpoint from the process of evaluative reflection

- opening up thinking to the infinite and to paradox; cultivating a feeling for the suprasensory

- experiencing the overcoming of darkness, pain, and resignation through acceptance of self

GRADE 12

Having officially come of age, the 18– to 19–year-old is the bearer of a basic inner question: "How can I make a difference in the social, economic, technological, and political conditions of the times? What is my role in all of this?"

In Grade 12 the intention is a grand tableau, a large-scale summing-up of the whole twelve years of schooling, with the Waldorf school's most significant educational idea at its heart: namely, the central position of the human being and his or her responsibility for the earth as an integral part of the cosmos. This points to the cross-disciplinary nature of the year's work. Whatever judgments the students come to now arise from comprehensive perspectives and from critical evaluation of the assumptions on which they are based. The aim is for them to arrive at their own interpretations, or their own practical reasoning.

The task for *biology* is to bring the topics covered in the preceding years together into a comprehensive overview. Here biology covers two large themes: the botany of the higher plants, and the zoology of the whole animal kingdom with particular orientation toward the human being. This entails, partly through detailed examples and partly through general descriptions, tracing the question of evolution from the simplest organisms to the human being.

Geography also has a synthesizing role. The cultural diversity of humanity in conjunction with sociopolitical and economic actualities may be taken as a main topic. This involves continuing the theme of globalization, but now with a view to understanding the spiritual currents through which the earth receives its human imprint.

Social studies has the same point of departure. The existence of the global economy means that it is important, on the one hand, to study the nature and function of money or the modern financial system, and, on the other, to become familiar with the concepts necessary to unmask the workings of international politics (analysis of actual crises and strategies). In conjunction with this, it is desirable to consider emerging possibilities and alternatives for the realization of civil societies based on justice, human dignity, and ecological and social responsibility.

On a similar note, in *foreign language lessons* the Grade 12 students should learn to appreciate the style of thought and expression peculiar to each language, and to integrate the cultural achievements typical of a particular country into an intercultural context. In this way they can, on the one hand, become aware of how diverse cultural forms are and, on the other, through understanding the foreign language and culture, develop a deeper understanding.

One main aim in *music* is to arrive at a description, appreciation, and understanding of the tonal language of contemporary music. In this way the students are challenged to emancipate themselves from their established listening habits and open themselves to new aesthetic experiences.

In *language arts* the work consists of a survey of literary history right up to the present. This is intended to enable the students to comprehend literature as a mirror of the development of human consciousness. The survey should not stop at the borders of the students' native language, but should extend into world literature. Engaging in this way with the modern image of the human being can culminate in an intensive study of the American transcendentalists or Goethe's *Faust*, a drama that provides the possibility of encountering the modern scientific worldview, its achievements and limitations, and also of exploring the limits of human consciousness. This in no way precludes taking a work of comparable thematic breadth and depth from some other area of world literature.

A certain parallel to the subjects of geography and one's native language is evident in what Steiner says about the *history* curriculum. A survey of world history should lead to the realization that we are members of one human world, and that our own position in history owes much to the cultural contribution of other peoples. An appreciation of one's own position in the present arises when this is understood as a phase in a developmental process, and the deeper layers in this process are uncovered. A concerted attempt is made to create an understanding for the many different ways cultures form and develop. Focusing on particular themes, major issues of modern times are considered, right up to the present: for instance, the issue of the structure of the social order (associated with problems of globalization), the issue of our attitude toward nature (technology and the environment), and the issue of the true nature of the human being (human rights, freedom of conscience).

Thinking about history should be taken as far as questioning, in philosophical or epistemological terms, the nature of the historical process itself. The teaching of history should not promote the feeling of being at the mercy of anonymous powers, but should encourage the conviction that by taking hold of new ideas, the self-motivated individual can influence the future and thus be a part of historical change. Events on the surface of history are examined symptomatically as indicators of deeper streams. Just as a physician looks as individual symptoms as indicators of underlying conditions by placing them in the context of the entire body, a history teacher helps the students develop a sense for the appearance of general and universal principles as they surface through significant events or moments in history.

Social studies in Grade 12 seeks to address diverse and multi-layered inter-relationships, both within the topics considered and among the inner faculties of the students (cognition, empathy, desire for action). The reciprocal effects between the economy, politics, and culture (and their corresponding ideals of solidarity or collaboration in economic life, equality in political life, and freedom or self-determination in cultural life), between the individual, the community, and the environment thus constitute a guideline and a testing ground for the development of a broad, critical social awareness. With this new-found power of discernment, the students are ready to be confronted with the full complexity of the human condition. These young adults should be capable of coping, in a constructive way, with the contradictions of earthly existence.

Added to this are the practical imperatives of becoming "grown up," which means emnbracing the responsibility associated with being old enough to work and to vote. It is the job of social studies to highlight the fact that this feeling of responsibility is applicable across the board, in all subject areas. In keeping with the thinking underlying Waldorf education, personal identity should develop in a spirit of respect for the dignity and beliefs of others and be based upon knowledge, awareness, and self-motivated action.

In *chemistry* too the aim is to offer something of a culminating summary. The work is centered upon the proteins, whereby a clear distinction can be made between plant and animal substance. The topics of crude oil as a by-product of protein breakdown and organic chemistry are also covered, as are the chemistry of nuclear processes and the threat they pose to life worldwide. Steiner's recommendation to consider the distinctions between dead and living organic as well as sentient animal and human substance is also taken up.

In *information technology* the themes dealt with are artificial intelligence, virtual reality, and implant technology. Besides further increasing technological understanding, the main consideration is a critical appraisal of technological developments in relation to their effects on society and the individual.

Physics begins with an experiential investigation of optical phenomena, the results of which are then used as examples from which to derive physical explanatory models. The applicability of quantum theory to the microcosmic and of relativity theory to the macrocosmic is juxtaposed with a human-oriented mode of apprehension. Using observation and facts arrived at by thinking things through, the attempt is made to find an approach to the nature of light.

In parallel to this, in *painting* and *modeling*, a hands-on, phenomenological study of Goethe's color theory can be undertaken. In addition, there is the possibility of doing pictorial and sculptural studies of the human head, the part of the body through which individuality expresses itself most clearly. Working in paint, clay, or stone, the student gives "his" or "her" head an unmistakably individual bone structure and a facial expression full of character. Disharmonies or "defects" in the form lead to questions like: "Is the human body an expression of the soul and spirit?"

In *eurythmy* something similar is attempted. The task is to find the form that corresponds to the fundamental gesture of a piece of music or a poem, so that in the performance the uniqueness, the inner quality of the work of art becomes visible. In their eurythmy performance, which is the culmination of this work, the students should be able to demonstrate that they are capable of bringing their personality to expression in form and movement.

The task facing the students in *mathematics* is to find an empirical path to integral and differential calculus out of purely numerical analysis. Generating threshold values as an infinite sequence leads them into working with ideas seemingly beyond the limits of the immediately perceptible. Threshold values of sequences can then be construed as representative substitutes of a continuous process. In developing the concept of the "differential quotient," the students should be in a position to grasp a new dimension of mathematics: the quotient of two differential sequences both tending toward zero generates something entirely new. They should get to the point not only of being able to apply this idea, but of knowing what it means in terms of real experience. Only now is the graphic display of the mathematical procedure added to the picture. Thus, the attempt is made to induce inner activity and a sense for the qualitative aspect of mathematics, which is ultimately essential if one is to feel at home in applied physics. In the exploration of the fundamentals of integral calculus, the students should come to see that in the realm of higher mathematics, one kind of procedure (differentiation) has its polar counterpart, which in turn opens up a further new level.

In a second math main lesson, depending on the point reached in Grade 11, projective geometry can be taken a stage further in the direction of affine diagrams. Two options are recommended: either the geometry of regular curves, or vector geometry. A further possibility for a second main lesson is to combine mathematics, botany, astronomy, embryology, and geometry into a grand, comprehensive picture.

Should a *social practicum* be undertaken this year, questions can be raised concerning the human condition, the manifestations of human dignity and the currents of destiny, especially in relation to people in need of care or restricted by some disability. If an ***industrial or job-shadowing practicum*** is undertaken, the students not only have the chance of getting to know economic life from the ground up, but they also experience what it means to be working together with other people in the service of a common economic goal. They also gain first-hand knowledge of the opportunities and problems associated with the modern division of labor. They get to observe, for instance, how a mistake at one work station affects the whole production process. And they learn just how much personal effort it takes to stay true to oneself and one's own standards in the juggling act between work and free time.

The responsibility of the individual to the community, and the knowledge that through everyone's combined efforts toward a common goal more is achieved than through the sum of each person's particular capabilities, are both made abundantly clear by the **Grade 12 play**. By joining forces around a full-scale play, opera, musical, cabaret, etc., the students have the opportunity—one last time—to experience one another as part of a class community. Speech, gesture, music, song, possibly eurythmy, staging, set design and construction, lighting, programming, and publicity (posters etc.)—all this must be worked out, coordinated, and brought to a grand culmination.

In keeping with the Grade 12 signature of choosing universal and complementary perspectives, the main theme of ***art history*** is architecture, which is a synthesis of all the fine and practical arts. Here it is not simply a question of following historical changes of style, but rather of looking at how different kinds of spatial structures and settlements express certain stages in the history of consciousness and social development. Art appreciation should by now be a way of arriving at a deeper understanding of the meaning and purpose of art; philosophizing about art (aesthetics) is now an important theme. An architecture main lesson in conjunction with an art field trip can create a practical and theoretical fusion of many subject areas of the Grade 12 year.

If Waldorf schools conduct their own final exams, the following is a possibility: every student chooses and executes a ***project*** that incorporates both a practical-artistic and a theoretical (cross-disciplinary) theme. The work is spread over the whole year in addition to normal lessons, and each of the two components is supervised by a mentor. The practical or artistic elements are all publicly displayed, either in the form of an exhibition or a performance. For the theoretical part, every student is required to give a public talk followed by discussion. Making an appropriate occasion of these presentations is all part of the organizational demands of the Grade 12 year.

The completion of this school year rounds off the twelve years of Waldorf education, the aim of which is to promote the emergence of "the truly human." In 1920 Steiner formulated this as follows:

> "Seek in your own being
> And you will find the world;
> Seek in world wide being
> And you will find yourself."

The intentions underlying the Grade 12 year

The basic aim is to learn to discern qualities from empirical observation, from actual phenomena; to take the step from the particular to the general. This entails:

- developing relational thinking, establishing meaningful connections, thereby coming to an understanding of the intelligent lawfulness of the world; generating ideas through synthesis

- being able to elucidate the interplay between idea and percept, form and matter

- following processes both forward and backward as an exercise of inner activity

- progressing from a causal-analytical to a teleological, or dynamically reflective way of approaching phenomena; learning to see law, necessity, freedom, and responsibility as aspects of a whole; likewise, seeing the relationship between human beings and nature, as well as human beings and society (part and whole), which in turn entails:

  - learning to deal with open questions, polarities, and contradictions

  - becoming aware of the assumptions behind one's own judgments

  - being prepared to make an active contribution to the world; taking a stand

Further aims:

- to engage with the question of personal destiny, bringing up issues surrounding the past and future of humanity

- to formulate relevant questions, practice re-thinking ideas and explanations, and develop the basic requirements for lifelong learning

Preparing Grade 12 for state examinations

In many countries, from Grade 10 on it is common practice for Waldorf students to begin preparing themselves for a finishing certificate of some kind, most notably state examinations. In preparing for these examinations, teachers are encouraged to use every opportunity to engage the students with deeper personal and social questions, so that the essence of Waldorf education is maintained even in an examination year. The 13th year, for instance, is not merely concerned with preparing for a state Abitur, matura, matric, or A-level exams, which happen essentially "outside" the Waldorf school curriculum; rather, this year continues to address the demands of society and challenges of the world. In other words, even during this exam year, the process of personality development, begun and nurtured in the preceding years of the students' education, continues to the end of their time in the Waldorf school.

INTEGRATION OF VOCATIONAL TRAINING; DIVERSIFICATION OF THE HIGH SCHOOL (A WORK IN PROGRESS)

Steiner's idea of cultural renewal through educational reform was an essential element in the original motivation behind the creation of Waldorf education. When he founded the first Waldorf school in 1919 as the educational expression of a campaign for social reform, his goal was a school that would provide solid preparation for life. His motto was: "Relevance to practical life is the hallmark of all teaching." (Steiner 1991: GA 192, p. 98) In this connection Steiner was doubtless also thinking of the teaching of practical subjects that would take place in workshops and result in the production of objects of everyday usefulness, which could then be sold. In work he saw a process of human development both on an individual and social level. In working—unfolding capabilities in the process—and making useful products, the human being in turn opens up the potential for similar action on the part of others.

On 3 August 1919, just before the training course for the first Waldorf teachers began, Steiner issued a rallying call: "To work is to learn! Working and learning belong together!" (Steiner: GA 192, p. 347) Four years after the founding of the Waldorf school he emphatically reiterated this claim: "And if one is able to answer in practical terms the great question of how a child's play can gradually be transformed into work, one has in effect answered the fundamental question of primary education." (Steiner 1989: GA 306, p. 76) Here an essential point is that learning happens more efficiently, and is in fact more fun, when the activity through which it occurs is direct and hands-on. This is particularly the case when the outcome of the learning process is a useful product, which might even be admired and purchased.

The crafts curriculum for the elementary school has been in development since the beginning of Waldorf education. With a view to its cultural and work-creating effects, it leads from a training in basic skills to a more advanced training in the form of apprenticeship. Practical training and cognitive learning are initially separated into a dual curriculum, then re-combined by means of artistic learning into a holistic education.

In high school, practicums place students in actual work situations where basic work experience and rudimentary professional skills can be acquired. The intention here is always to integrate personal development, creativity, and acquired technical skill into a future-oriented preparation for a professional path.

BIBLIOGRAPHY

As in the German edition, references to Rudolf Steiner's writings are listed separately from other sources. German titles of these writings are being left untranslated because many of the books cited here have not been rendered into English; furthermore, some that have been published in English have appeared under multiple titles. The Rosetta Stone to using this list of references, therefore, is the number of the GA [*Gesamtausgabe* or Collected Works], which is the same in both German and—if they exist—English publications.

WORKS BY RUDOLF STEINER

Steiner, R. (GA 9): *Theosophie*. Dornach, 1995

Steiner, R. (GA 23): *Die Kernpunkte der sozialen Frage*. Dornach, 1976

Steiner, R. (GA 24): Freie Schule und Dreigliederung. In: *Aufsätze über die Dreigliederung des sozialen Organismus und zur Zeitlage 1915–1921*. Dornach, 1982

Steiner, R. /Wegman, I. (GA 27): *Grundlegendes für eine Erweiterung der Heilkunst nach geisteswissenschaftlichen Erkenntnissen*. Dornach, 1991

Steiner, R. (GA 31): *Gesammelte Aufsätze zur Kultur- und Zeitgeschichte 1887–1901*. Dornach, 1989

Steiner, R. (GA 34): *Lucifer – Gnosis. Grundlegende Aufsätze zur Anthroposophie*. Dornach, 1987

Steiner, R. (GA 36): *Der Goetheanumgedanke inmitten der Kulturkrisis der Gegenwart.* Dornach, 1976
Steiner, R. (GA 40): *Wahrspruchworte.* Dornach, 2005
Steiner, R. (GA 192): *Geisteswissenschaftliche Behandlung sozialer und pädagogischer Fragen.* Dornach, 1964
Steiner, R. (GA 217): *Geistige Wirkenskräfte im Zusammenleben von alter und junger Generation. Pädagogischer Jugendkurs.* Dornach, 1979
Steiner, R. (GA 293): *Allgemeine Menschenkunde als Grundlage der Pädagogik.* Dornach, 1992
Steiner, R. (GA 294): *Erziehungskunst. Methodisch-Didaktisches.* Dornach, 1990
Steiner, R. (GA 295): *Erziehungskunst. Seminarbesprechungen und Lehrplanvorträge.* Dornach, 1984
Steiner, R. (GA 296): *Die Erziehungsfrage als soziale Frage.* Dornach, 1979
Steiner, R. (GA 300): *Konferenzen mit den Lehrern der Freien Waldorfschule 1919 bis 1924.* Dornach, 1975
Steiner, R. (GA 301): *Die Erneuerung der pädagogisch-didaktischen Kunst durch Geisteswisseschaft.* Dornach, 1991
Steiner, R. (GA 302): *Menschenerkenntnis und Unterrichtsgestaltung.* Dornach, 1986
Steiner, R. (GA 302a):*Erziehung und Unterricht aus Menschenerkenntnis.* Dornach, 1993
Steiner, R. (GA 303): *Die gesunde Entwicklung des Menschenwesens. Eine Einführung in die anthroposophische Pädagogik und Didaktik.* Dornach, 1987
Steiner, R. (GA 304): *Erziehungs- und Unterrichtsmethoden auf anthroposophischer Grundlage.* Dornach, 1979
Steiner, R. (GA 304a): *Anthroposophische Menschenkunde und Pädagogik.* Dornach, 1979
Steiner, R. (GA 305): *Die geistig-seelischen Grundkräfte der Erziehungskunst. Spirituelle Werte in Erziehung und sozialem Leben.* Dornach, 1991
Steiner, R. (GA 306): *Die pädagogische Praxis vom Gesichtspunkte geisteswissenschaftlicher Menschenerkenntnis.* Dornach, 1982
Steiner, R. (GA 307): *Gegenwärtiges Geistesleben und Erziehung.* Dornach, 1986
Steiner, R. (GA 308): *Die Methodik des Lehrens und die Lebensbedingungen des Erziehens.* Dornach, 1986

Steiner, R. (GA 309): *Anthroposophische Pädagogik und ihre Voraussetzungen.* Dornach, 1981
Steiner, R. (GA 310): *Der pädagogische Wert der Menschenerkenntnis und der Kulturwert der Pädagogik.* Dornach, 1965
Steiner, R. (GA 311): *Die Kunst des Erziehens aus dem Erfassen der Menschenwesenheit.* Dornach, 1979
Steiner, R. (GA 317): *Heilpädagogischer Kurs.* Dornach, 1985

WORKS CITED BY OTHER AUTHORS
Foreword
Buber, M. (1969): *Reden über Erziehung.* Heidelberg
On the Publication of this Guide
Heydebrand, C. v. (1994): *Vom Lehrplan der Freien Waldorfschule.* Stuttgart
Part I Tasks and Objectives of Waldorf Education

The Curriculum in its Anthroposophical Context
Kiersch, J. (2010): «*Mit ganz andern Mitteln gemalt*». *Überlegungen zur hermeneutischen Erschließung der esoterischen Lehrerkurse Rudolf Steiners.* In: RoSE Vol. I, No. II, p. 73–82.
Kranich, E.-M. (1998): *Anthropologische Grundlagen der Waldorfpädagogik.* Stuttgart
Kranich, E.-M. (2003): *Der innere Mensch und sein Leib. Eine Anthropologie.* Stuttgart
Leber, S. (1989): *Weltanschauung, Ideologie und Schulwesen.* Stuttgart
Leber, S. (1993): *Die Menschenkunde der Waldorfpädagogik.* Stuttgart
Rittelmeyer, C. (2002): *Die pädagogische Anthropologie des Leibes.* Weinheim
Wulf, C. / Zirfas, J. (2014): *Handbuch Pädagogische Anthropologie.* Berlin

Administration through Community Participation
Dietz, K. M. (2006): *Dialogische Schulführung an Waldorfschulen.* Heidelberg
Lindenberg, Christoph: *Rudolf Steiner. Eine Biographie.* Band II, Stuttgart 1997, S. 676 ff.

Teaching and Learning Processes

Beer, G. / Schwarz, W. (2012): Lernen und Bewegung – Schlaglichter auf den aktuellen Forschungsstand. In: *Erziehung und Unterricht*. Jänner/Februar 1–2, Wien

Brunner, I. (2002): Zielorientiertes Lernen und persönliche Bestleistung. Portfolios als Hilfe zum selbstgesteuerten Lernen in der Grundstufe. In: *ide – Informationen zur Deutschdidaktik*. Heft 1/02, Innsbruck

Carle, M. (2014): *Lernen in Bewegung* www.waldorfideenpool.de, Schulkonzepte/das Bochumer Modell/ das bewegliche Klassenzimmer/Lernen in Bewegung

Finke, H. (2016): Die Goetheanistische Methode und ihre Anwendung im Unterricht der Waldorfschule. In Weiss, L. / Willmann, C. (Hrsg): *Erziehung im Dialog, Jahrbuch für Waldorfpädagogik*. Gudjons, H. (2011): *Frontalunterricht – neu entdeckt: Integration in offene Unterrichtsformen*. Stuttgart

Harslem, M. / Randoll, D. (2013): *Selbstverantwortliches Lernen an Freien Waldorfschulen*. Frankfurt/M

Iwan, R. (2005): *Zeig, was du kannst! Portfolioarbeit als zentrales Anliegen der Waldorfpädagogik*. Heidelberg

Lichtenberg, G. C. (1958): *Aphorismen*. Zürich

Rosslenbroich, B. (1994): Die *rhythmische Organisation des Menschen. Aus der chronobiologischen Forschung*. Stuttgart

Ruf, U. / Gallin, P. (2011): *Dialogisches Lernen in Sprache und Mathematik*. Velber

Schad, W. (1991): *Erziehung ist Kunst*. Stuttgart

Schieren, J. (2010): Die goetheanistische Bewusstseinshaltung der Waldorfpädagogik. In Paschen, H. (Hrsg.): *Erziehungswissenschaftliche Zugänge zur Waldorfpädagogik*. Wiesbaden

Schiller, F. (2000): *Über die ästhetische Erziehung des Menschen*. Reclam, Nr. 18062, Stuttgart

Schneider, P. (1982): *Einführung in die Waldorfpädagogik*. Stuttgart

Wagenschein, M. (1968): *Verstehen lehren*. Basel

Wiehl, A. (2015): *Propädeutik der Unterrichtsmethoden in der Waldorfpädagogik*, Frankfurt am Main

Part II The Waldorf Curriculum Viewed Horizontally Grades 1–12

Horizontal and Vertical Curriculum: A Comparison

Rittelmeyer, C. (2010): Vorwort in: Paschen, H. (Hrsg.), *Erziehungswissenschaftliche Zugänge zur Waldorfpädagogik*. Wiesbaden

Background to Teaching in the Elementary-School Grades

Antonovsky, A. (1993): Gesundheitsforschung versus Krankheitsforschung. In: A. Franke/M. Broda (Hrsg.): *Psychosomatische Gesundheit*. Tübingen

Antonovsky, A. (1997): *Salutogenese. Zur Entmystifizierung der Gesundheit*. Tübingen

Fucke, E. (1993): *Grundlinien einer Pädagogik des Jugendalters. Zur Lehrplankonzeption der Klassen 6 bis 10 an Waldorfschulen*. Stuttgart

Gebser, J. (1986): *Ursprung und Gegenwart. Die Fundamente der aperspektivischen Welt*. München

Götte, W. / Loebell, P. / Maurer, K.-M. (2009): *Entwicklungsaufgaben und Kompetenzen. Zum Bildungs-plan der Waldorfschule*. Stuttgart

Honig, M.-S. (2002): Geschichte der Kindheit. In: Krüger, H.-H. / Grunert, C. (Hrsg.): *Handbuch Kindheits- und Jugendforschung*. Opladen

Loebell, P. (2010): Die Signaturen der menschlichen Entwicklung als Grundlage der Waldorfpädagogik. In: Paschen, H.: *Erziehungswissenschaftliche Zugänge zur Waldorfpädagogik*. Wiesbaden

Leber, S. (1993): *Die Menschenkunde der Waldorfpädagogik. Anthropologische Grundlagen der Erziehung des Kindes und Jugendlichen*. Stuttgart

Knußmann, R. (1996): *Vergleichende Biologie des Menschen*. Stuttgart u. a.

Kranich, E.-M. (1999): *Anthropologische Grundlagen der Waldorfpädagogik*. Stuttgart

Pehm. R. (2015): *Das Neue gewinnen, ohne das Alte aufzugeben? Der Umgang mit der «Schulreife» an waldorfpädagogischen Einrichtungen in Österreich*. (Hrsg.) Zentrum für Kultur und Pädagogik, Wien

Pädagogische Sektion am Goetheanum (Hrsg.) (2013): *Themenheft Schulreife*. Dornach

Schiller, H. (2005): Das Kind in der mittleren Klassenlehrerzeit. In: *Zur Unterrichtsgestaltung im 1. bis 8. Schuljahr an Waldorf-/Rudolf-Steiner-Schulen [sic]*. Dornach

Ullrich, H. (2010): Das Konzept der Kindheit – ein aktuelles Problemfeld der Waldorfpädagogik. In Paschen, H. *Erziehungswissenschaftliche Zugänge zur Waldorfpädagogik*. Wiesbaden

Wagner, H. / Ehm, J.-H. / Hasselhorn, M. (2010) «Schulreifes Kind». Individuelle Voraussetzungen für den Schulstart optimieren, In: *Lehren und Lernen* 36 (3). Villingen-Schwenningen

Horizontal Curriculum of the Elementary-School Years

Brater, M. / Munz, C. (1994): *Die pädagogische Bedeutung der Buchführung.* Stuttgart

Buck, P. / Mackensen, M. v. (1990): *Naturphänomene erlebend verstehen.* Köln

Bühler, E. et al. (2000): *Formenzeichnen. Die Entwicklung des Formensinns in der Erziehung.* Stuttgart

Fucke, E. (1993): *Grundlinien einer Pädagogik des Jugendalters. Zur Lehrplankonzeption der Klassen 6 bis 10 an Waldorfschulen.* Stuttgart

Grohmann, G. (1992): *Zur ersten Tier- und Pflanzenkunde in der Pädagogik Rudolf Steiners.* Stuttgart

Herder, J. G. (1989): *Der Mensch ist der erste Freigelassene der Schöpfung. Aus den ersten fünf Büchern der «Ideen zur Philosophie der Geschichte des Menschen».* Stuttgart

Kandinsky, W. (1952): *Über das Geistige in der Kunst.* Bern

Müller-Wiedemann, H. (1999): *Mitte der Kindheit. Das neunte bis zwölfte Lebensjahr. Beiträge zu einer anthroposophischen Entwicklungspsychologie.* Stuttgart

Schuberth, E. (2008): *Das Formenzeichnen als tätige Geometrie.* Stuttgart

Wilson, F. R. (2000): *Die Hand – Geniestreich der Evolution.* Stuttgart

Background to the High-School Curriculum

Fischer, W. (1966): *Der junge Mensch.* Freiburg

Fucke, E. (1993): *Grundlinien einer Pädagogik des Jugendalters. Zur Lehrplankonzeption der Klassen 6 bis 10 an Waldorfschulen.* Stuttgart

Kranich, E.-M. in Bohnsack, F. / Kranich, E.-M. (Hrsg.) (1990): *Erziehungswissenschaft und Waldorfpädagogik.* Weinheim/Basel

Piaget, J. (1974): *Theorien und Methoden der modernen Erziehung.* Frankfurt

The High-School Years

Schirmer, H. (1993): *Bildekräfte der Dichtung. Zum Literaturunterricht der Oberstufe.* Stuttgart

ACKNOWLEDGEMENTS

A great number of people were involved in the making of this book, and to them many thanks are due:

First and foremost to Alexander Hassenstein, who was responsible for coordinating the project at the behest of the *Pädagogische Forschungsstelle beim Bund der Freien Waldorfschulen*. His meticulous planning and organizational skills kept the numerous authors involved on target.

The editorial board—consisting of Christian Boettger, Claus-Peter Röh, Michael Zech, and myself—worked together as a harmonious team. Our interactions were reliably stimulating, amicably critical, and agreeably objective. For their extraordinary level of commitment—both in their attention to detail and broad awareness of the whole—they deserve heartfelt thanks. The conversations of this team focused on discovering what lay behind the established content of the curriculum, with the intention of finding ways to express the visionary aspects of Rudolf Steiner's educational ideas. These were conversations truly inspired by the Waldorf curriculum.

I would also like to thank the many colleagues who contributed articles, supplementary material, and helpful suggestions. Without their support this project would not have been possible. The names of the writers and the subject areas they were responsible for can be found in the bibliography at the end of this volume.

As a representative of those many colleagues involved in the first edition of this guide to the Waldorf curriculum, I feel compelled to sound the name of Stefan Leber. At a meeting of the "Hague Circle" (now called the International Forum for Steiner/Waldorf Education) in 1992, it was he who posed the question whether—after nearly 75 years of Waldorf education—it was time for the schools to publish a clear and comprehensive statement of their activities in the form of a curriculum guide.

He was also the one to articulate need for such a curriculum project despite a "storm of protests" that initially greeted the suggestion—which is to say, he gave me the support I needed to carry out this task. For this, I thank him most heartily.

— *Tobias Richter*
Vienna, March 2015

Made in the USA
Middletown, DE
24 November 2020